BALANCING CUSTOMER EXPECTATIONS "THE TRUTH UNVEILED"

"A GUIDE UNCOVERING THE REALITIES OF MANAGING CUSTOMER RELATIONSHIPS, BALANCING RESPECT AND BOUNDARIES FOR LASTING TRUST."

JAGADEESAN SUBRAMANIAN

Made with ♥ on the Notion Press Platform
www.notionpress.com

This book is dedicated to Mohammed Al Sulaimi, whose insights during our discussions inspired me to write it. He encouraged me to reflect on and share the lessons I've learned over the years from managing relationships in both my personal and professional life.

Contents

Epigraph

True understanding comes not from treating customers as deities, but as partners in mutual growth and respect. In both personal and professional realms, relationships are strengthened when empathy and fairness guide our actions. A balanced approach acknowledges the customer's value without compromising our integrity. It's through this balance that trust is built and loyalty is forged. Let us remember: customers are vital, but so is the courage to set boundaries. In partnership, not reverence, lies the path to meaningful connections.

Foreword

Mahesh Gandhi

Founder & Managing Director, Apodis Hotels & Resorts.

I have known Jagadeesan Subramanian in a very different capacity. I and our colleagues always called him YesJ. In a sense, the word YES symbolises the entire effort behind this book by Jagadeesan. YesJ met me when we set up affordable kitchens and service lines for F and B in one of our early ventures, setting up a chain of affordable/ budget hotels. He rolled up his sleeves and plunged with gusto sharing the same spirit with his Team in completing the projects in time and cost.

He is multi-skilled, multidisciplined and always restless moving between assignments where he could expand his learning and deliver the learning. He has remained humble and strong a family man who shows up in the early segmentation of who is a customer. It came as no surprise therefore that YesJ wrote this book on Customer Relationships exploring how respect and trust are two sides of the coin that are most times invisible to the customer. In the concluding pages, there are references to AI and AIE to which I would add Augmented Intelligence. Augmented Intelligence could be useful in mapping and analysing customer feedback. Early use of Chatbots and similar score well on standard information references for routine and repetitive tasks.

From a customer viewpoint application of Tech presently sits between Hype and Reality as each customer comes with different expectations as only humans are not die-cast.

I am sure this book will be immensely useful even to well-read followers of customer-centricity

Happy reading.

Preface

In a world where the phrase "the customer is always right" has become a mantra, I invite you to take a step back and reconsider its full implications. While customer satisfaction is undeniably crucial, it is equally important to approach interactions with balance and fairness, both in professional and personal relationships. This book, Balancing Customer Expectations – The Truth Unveiled, delves into the nuanced understanding of customers as partners rather than infallible figures. It explores the principles that guide meaningful relationships, emphasizes the importance of setting boundaries, and highlights the rewards of cultivating genuine connections based on respect and mutual benefit.

My journey in writing this book began through a thought-provoking discussion with Mohammed Al Sulaimi, who inspired me to document the insights I gained over years of working with diverse individuals. From navigating professional challenges to handling delicate personal interactions, I have experienced first-hand the importance of treating each encounter with integrity, empathy, and clarity. Through these pages, I aim to share strategies that empower individuals to manage relationships with confidence, recognizing the distinct qualities of genuine and toxic customers, and implementing systems that foster positive growth and loyalty.

Whether you are a leader striving for excellence in your field or someone looking to strengthen personal connections, this book offers guidance and practical advice to help you achieve a balanced, fulfilling approach to managing expectations. The learning and insight I gained over years from various situations and people are compiled for the benefit of the readers. If there are any disagreements, they might arise from the differences in perspective and thinking. Do not force yourself to indulge in conflict, as this work is written solely with the intention of benefiting people and fostering a mindset rooted in positivity.

Acknowledgements

Entire teachers and team of The Boys Higher Secondary School, Srirangam. For guiding me to be a good person.

Entire college team of IHMCT, Goa. For guiding me to become a thorough professional and Mr. Jyjoe Thomas, my friend, who helped me overcome challenges during college and afterward.

To Mr. Annadurai and Mr. Antoine, who has played an important role in my life by guiding me in various aspects of life.

To the children of my friends, well-wishers, and myself, Ayusi, Calvin, Cassya, Daksh, Darsini, Dhayalini Vivek, Dinesh Kumar, Evelyn, Harita Varssyni, Idhayanidhi, Ishanvi, Jean Roderick, Joanna, Joel, Jordan. Joshua, Keanu Antonio, Melvin Frederick, Poornima Jesudason, Prithvi, Rajalakshmi, Siddhved, Snehan Viviek, Sreekrishnan, Vagula, Vardhan, Vikram, Vemakshi, Kavya and Sarveshvaran.

Durai Dyanidhi is a special person in our family, whom we adore and wish a happy and healthy life always.

Prologue

In an age where customer-centricity reigns supreme, we often hear the adage, “The customer is always right.” While this sentiment captures the essence of valuing our customers, it can lead to misunderstandings and unrealistic expectations. As we navigate the complexities of both personal and professional relationships, it becomes evident that this mantra requires a more nuanced interpretation. Customers, like all individuals, are multifaceted beings who bring their own perspectives, needs, and emotions into every interaction.

In this book, I invite you on a journey to explore the delicate balance between meeting customer expectations and upholding the integrity of our relationships. Drawing from years of experience in dealing with a diverse array of individuals, I aim to unveil the truths that underpin effective communication, trust, and mutual respect. Together, we will dissect the various types of customers we encounter—both genuine and toxic—and examine the principles that guide us in handling these relationships with grace and understanding.

This work is not just for business leaders or customer service professionals; it is for anyone seeking to cultivate meaningful connections in their personal lives as well. The insights shared within these pages are born from real-world interactions and reflections, aiming to provide practical tools and strategies for fostering a culture of collaboration and empathy.

As we delve into the chapters ahead, I encourage you to keep an open mind and consider the perspectives presented. Each interaction, whether in business or in life, offers an opportunity for growth and learning. By embracing this mindset, we can transform challenges into stepping stones towards building a more compassionate and supportive community.

Let us embark on this exploration together, as we uncover the truths behind customer expectations and the art of balancing them with the fundamental principles of respect and kindness.

CHAPTER ONE

Everyone is our Customer

The Importance of Viewing Everyone as a Customer:

Cultivating Respect and Harmony in Life

In a world where interactions shape our daily experiences, it is invaluable to adopt a mindset that sees everyone we meet as a potential customer. This is not to suggest that every interaction involves a financial transaction or that relationships are commodified. Instead, this perspective emphasizes the idea that every person we encounter deserves to be treated with the same respect, attention, and understanding that we would offer to a customer in a business setting. The profound impact of this mindset goes beyond professional gain; it enhances our personal growth, enriches our relationships, and fosters a community grounded in mutual respect and harmony.

The Principle of Respect Amid Challenges

Life often presents us with challenging interactions. Whether it's a colleague whose opinions clash with ours, a friend who acts inconsiderately, or a stranger who tests our patience, such moments can provoke frustration or irritation. In these instances, our natural response may lean toward defensiveness or anger. However, by choosing to treat these individuals as we would a valued customer—calmly, respectfully, and without harsh words—we take control of the situation and elevate the quality of our interactions.

When customers in a professional setting express dissatisfaction, it is common practice to respond with understanding and solutions rather than anger or confrontation. This same principle applies to life outside of work. Maintaining a demeanour of respect, even when faced with challenging behaviour, helps to prevent escalation and creates an environment where productive dialogue can flourish. Speaking respectfully, even when provoked, sets a tone that can often lead the other person to reconsider their approach. This practice not only preserves the relationship but may inspire a shift in the other person's behaviour as well.

1. Customers are everyone and everywhere

The Ripple Effect of Treating Everyone as a Customer

Why is it important to consider everyone we come across as a customer? The answer lies in the benefits this approach brings to our interactions and relationships. When we view others through this lens, we are reminded of the inherent value each person holds. This mindset encourages us to see past the immediate frustrations of a moment and respond in a manner that nurtures respect and understanding.

By treating others with unwavering respect—even when their actions test our patience—we build relationships that are resilient and long-lasting. This approach does not mean ignoring our boundaries or excusing harmful behaviour; rather, it is about responding in a way that reflects our commitment to kindness and integrity. When we choose respectful communication, we demonstrate emotional maturity and set a standard for how we expect to be treated in return.

Over time, this consistent practice of respect can change how people interact with us. When someone realizes that we treat them with dignity regardless of the situation, they are more likely to adjust their behaviour positively. This effect, though subtle, can foster deeper connections and encourage a culture of understanding. It is a way to lead by example, showing that respect is not conditional on others' behaviour but a reflection of our own character.

The Power of Respectful Communication

Maintaining respect in all our interactions cultivates a profound skill: the ability to communicate effectively and lovingly. This skill becomes part of who we are, influencing how we respond in every conversation. Over time, we become experts in expressing ourselves with kindness, even when faced with conflict. Harsh or abusive language loses its place in our vocabulary, replaced by words that convey respect and empathy.

This transformation can be life-changing. By choosing words thoughtfully and avoiding reactive anger, we become more composed and approachable. Our reputation as individuals who can maintain their composure under pressure grows, and others come to appreciate us not just for what we say but for how we make them feel. This form of communication is rooted in love and compassion, strengthening our relationships and making us better partners, friends, colleagues, and community members.

Becoming a Lovelier Human Being

Adopting the principle of seeing everyone as a customer does more than improve relationships; it reshapes who we are. We evolve into individuals who radiate understanding and patience. This shift in behaviour reflects a deeper transformation in which respect becomes a core value that guides all interactions. We develop a habit of listening intently, responding thoughtfully, and prioritizing harmony over winning an argument or asserting dominance.

This commitment to respectful communication allows us to look back on our interactions with pride. We realize that we have become better versions of ourselves—not because we avoided conflict, but because we chose to handle it with grace. We become role models for those around us, exemplifying how choosing love and respect can strengthen connections and contribute to personal growth. In turn, this behaviour inspires others to adopt similar practices, creating a ripple effect that extends far beyond our immediate circles.

A Path to Harmony and Respect

Seeing everyone we meet as a customer is more than a mindset—it is a way of life that promotes harmony, mutual respect, and deeper connections. By choosing to treat others with the utmost respect, even in the face of frustration or irritation, we elevate our interactions and set the stage for more meaningful relationships. This approach teaches us to communicate with love and empathy, leaving behind harsh words and impulsive reactions.

As we continue on this path, we become more than just people who communicate well; we become individuals who embody kindness and compassion. We contribute to a culture of respect that enriches not only our lives but the lives of everyone we encounter. In doing so, we become proud of the person we are—a lovely human being who understands that true strength lies in choosing respect over retaliation and love over indifference.

CHAPTER TWO

Types of Customers

Understanding Customer Types in Life:

Professional and Personal Customers

In every aspect of our lives, we interact with various individuals who can be classified as customers. The term "customer" often conjures images of clients seeking products or services, but it extends far beyond this traditional definition. In fact, understanding the types of customers we encounter—internal and external—can enhance our interactions and strengthen our relationships, both professionally and personally. Broadly, we can categorize customers into two main types: professional customers and personal customers.

Professional Customers

Professional customers encompass individuals and entities engaged in business relationships. This includes clients, consumers, partners, and stakeholders who interact with a company in various capacities. In this context, understanding customer needs and expectations is critical for success. Businesses rely on their professional customers to sustain operations, generate revenue, and build brand loyalty.

Personal Customers

On the other hand, personal customers are individuals we encounter in our daily lives outside of a professional setting. This group includes family members, friends, acquaintances, and even strangers we meet in our communities. Each interaction with personal customers can enrich our lives and contribute to our social well-being. Recognizing the importance of these relationships fosters a supportive environment where kindness and respect thrive.

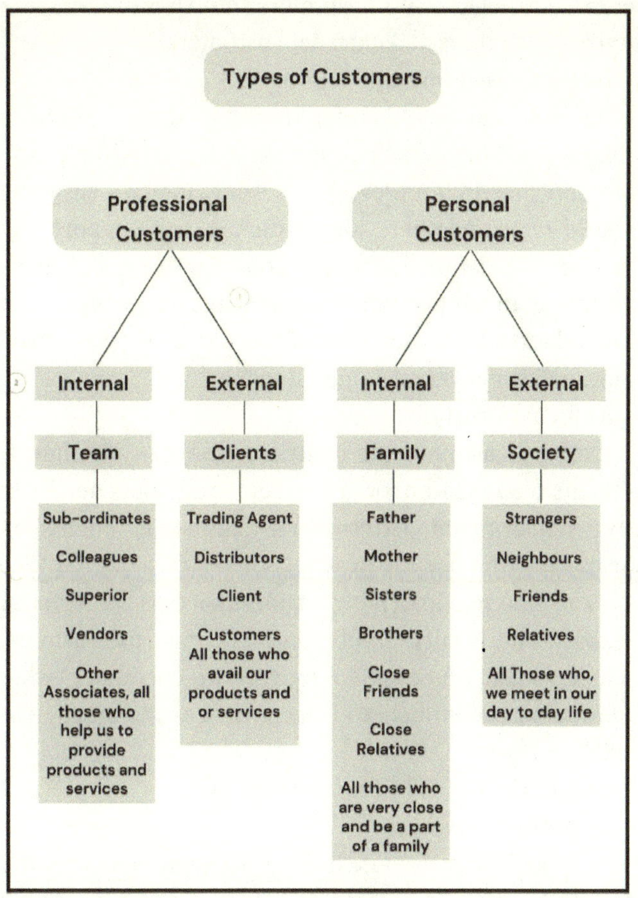

2. Types of Customers

Sub-types of Customers

Within both the professional and personal categories, we can further classify customers into two subcategories: internal customers and external customers.

Internal Customers

Internal customers refer to individuals within an organization or personal sphere who contribute to a common goal. In a professional setting, internal customers include team members, departments, and support staff. They are crucial for creating a collaborative and effective workplace. In our personal lives, internal customers are our close relationships, such as family and friends, who provide emotional support and companionship.

External Customers

External customers, in contrast, are those who interact with an organization or individual from outside. In the professional realm, external customers are clients and consumers who use the products or services offered. They play a pivotal role in driving business success through their feedback and loyalty. In personal life, external customers include acquaintances and strangers we encounter, whose interactions can influence our experiences and broaden our social networks.

Customer Types in Professional Life

Internal Customers

In a professional context, internal customers are those who work within an organization, including team members and support vendors. These individuals play a crucial role in the success of a business. Internal customers rely on one another to achieve shared goals and objectives, creating a collaborative environment that fosters productivity and innovation.

The importance of internal customers cannot be overstated. When team members communicate effectively and support each other, the entire organization benefits. Trust among colleagues leads to improved morale, enhanced teamwork, and a sense of belonging. To engage internal customers, organizations should implement strategies that encourage collaboration and open communication. Regular feedback sessions, team-building activities, and recognition of individual contributions can help create a positive work culture that values each member's input.

External Customers

In contrast, external customers are those who use or purchase a business's products or services. These individuals may include clients, consumers, or anyone seeking to benefit from what the organization offers. Engaging external customers is vital for a business's growth and sustainability, as their satisfaction directly impacts brand loyalty and market success.

Understanding the needs and preferences of external customers is essential for any organization. By actively listening to feedback and adapting to customer demands, businesses can build strong relationships with their clientele. Effective communication, timely responses, and a commitment to quality service are key components in fostering these connections. Companies that prioritize their external customers often enjoy enhanced reputation and increased customer retention.

Customer Types in Personal Life

Internal Customers

Beyond the workplace, the concept of internal customers also applies to our personal lives. Internal customers in this context are the close relationships we cherish—our family members, close friends, and loved ones. These individuals provide us with emotional support, companionship, and a sense of belonging.

The significance of nurturing internal relationships cannot be overlooked. Strong bonds with family and friends contribute to our overall well-being and happiness. To foster these connections, it is essential to communicate openly, share experiences, and spend quality time together. Celebrating milestones, offering support during challenging times, and simply being present for one another are vital practices that strengthen these internal ties.

External Customers

Conversely, external customers in our personal lives refer to those we encounter outside our close circle, including acquaintances, colleagues, and even strangers. While these relationships may not be as intimate, they are equally important in shaping our social experiences and community interactions.

Engaging with external customers in our daily lives requires a mindful approach. Treating everyone we meet with kindness and respect can lead to positive social interactions that enrich our lives. Simple gestures—like greeting a neighbour or offering assistance to a stranger—can create a ripple effect of goodwill in our communities. By acknowledging the value of these interactions, we open ourselves to new opportunities and relationships that enhance our social fabric.

The Significance of Valuing Relationships

Understanding the distinctions between internal and external customers is crucial for personal fulfilment and professional success. Each type of customer contributes to our lives in meaningful ways, and recognizing their significance can enhance our interactions. The dynamics of our relationships—whether close or distant—impact our mental health, happiness, and overall life satisfaction.

Moreover, kindness and respect should be the cornerstones of all interactions, regardless of whether someone is an internal or external customer. When we approach each relationship with empathy and understanding, we create a supportive environment that nurtures growth and connection. Positive interactions foster a sense of community and belonging, enriching both our personal and professional lives.

Beyond Business: The True Value of Customer

The concept of internal and external customers extends far beyond the realm of business. By recognizing and valuing these relationships in both professional and personal contexts, we can enhance our interactions and build a network of support and goodwill. Whether through fostering strong internal bonds with family and colleagues or treating external customers with respect and kindness, the way we engage with others shapes our experiences and contributes to a more fulfilling life. As we navigate our daily interactions, let us strive to embrace the essence of kindness and respect, ensuring that every customer—internal or external—feels valued and appreciated.

CHAPTER THREE

Understanding the Concept of Customers

Selling Ourselves in Personal Life

When we think of customers, our minds often gravitate toward the traditional notions of commerce, where businesses exchange products or services for money. In this context, customers are individuals or entities that purchase goods or services with specific expectations. This exchange creates a dynamic that drives economies and fosters innovation, as businesses strive to meet the needs of their clientele. However, this concept of customers extends beyond the marketplace and penetrates our personal lives in profound and meaningful ways. The idea that we "sell" something to our customers in personal life—essentially, ourselves—challenges us to rethink the nature of relationships and the value we provide to others.

Selling Ourselves: The Foundation of Relationships

In every interaction we have, whether with family, friends, or strangers, we are unconsciously engaging in a form of "selling" ourselves. This concept may seem surprising, yet it is the foundation of many of our relationships. Selling ourselves, in this context, is not about superficial charm or persuasive tactics; it's about offering the true essence of who we are—our values, emotions, and intentions—to others. This process of "selling" is not something that most people consciously recognize, but it happens in our everyday life, and it is integral to the relationships we build and sustain.

The Unseen Nature of Self-Selling

Unknowingly, each of us engages in this process of selling ourselves every day. When we interact with those around us, we showcase qualities like empathy, patience, trustworthiness, or humour. We "sell" these aspects of ourselves as a way to connect and form bonds. In doing so, we shape others' perceptions of us and influence how they respond to us. For instance, a warm smile, a helpful gesture, or genuine attentiveness can leave lasting impressions that deepen the foundation of a relationship.

However, because we don't fully understand the purpose and meaning of selling ourselves, we often miss the opportunity to intentionally cultivate the quality of our relationships. The way our minds work can lead us to behave on autopilot, acting and expressing ourselves reactively. We may respond in ways that are not aligned with our true intentions or values, which can inadvertently weaken our connections. This disconnect between intention and expression is one reason why relationships sometimes falter, despite our best efforts.

The Role of Purpose and Awareness in Building Relationships

When we approach relationships without understanding the purpose of selling ourselves, we often end up responding based on habits, assumptions, or emotional impulses. Without mindfulness, we may unknowingly project behaviours or attitudes that don't truly represent us, leaving others confused or disconnected. This can lead to misunderstandings and, ultimately, to missed opportunities for meaningful connection. Recognizing that each interaction is an opportunity to share our best qualities can help bridge this gap.

Being aware of our role in the relationship allows us to be more intentional in expressing ourselves. When we understand that we are, in effect, "selling" who we are in each interaction, we become more mindful of the energy, words, and emotions we bring into our relationships. This shift in perspective brings a sense of responsibility to ensure that what we convey is aligned with our values and the relationship we seek to cultivate. It is a way of maintaining integrity while connecting deeply with others, building relationships that are based on authenticity and mutual respect.

The Common Pitfalls and Why We Often Miss Relationship Opportunities

One of the key challenges in this process is recognizing that the mind's immediate responses are not always in line with our genuine intentions. For example, in moments of frustration or stress, we may react defensively or impatiently, leading others to perceive us in ways that don't reflect our true selves. These moments, if unchecked, can undermine the foundation of trust and respect within a relationship. Without an awareness of the "self-selling" process, we risk falling into patterns that can harm even our closest connections.

Another common pitfall is that people often approach relationships with expectations. We may "sell" ourselves in ways we think others want us to be, rather than showing who we genuinely are. This approach can create a superficial bond that lacks the strength to endure challenges. True relationships, like successful sales, are built on understanding, honesty, and a genuine interest in the other person's needs and values.

Turning Awareness into Action: Building Stronger Relationships

To avoid these pitfalls, we can turn our awareness into actionable habits that enhance our interactions. Recognizing the role we play in each relationship enables us to take responsibility for the quality of our connections. Here are some ways to practice intentional “self-selling”:

Self-Reflection: Regularly reflect on how you present yourself in different relationships. Are your actions and words aligned with your intentions? This practice will help you catch habits that might not serve your relationships and allow you to adjust.

Empathy and Understanding: Place yourself in the other person's shoes to understand their perspective. Empathy builds a bridge of trust and strengthens relationships, demonstrating that you genuinely care.

Consistent Integrity: Show up as your true self in every interaction. Honesty and consistency in your words and actions establish trust over time, which is the backbone of meaningful connections.

Adaptability: Relationships are dynamic, and our approach must adapt to each person's needs and context. Being flexible and responsive allows us to be more effective in nurturing the bonds we share.

Embracing the Purpose of Selling Ourselves

Selling ourselves is not an act of manipulation but a practice of intentional engagement. When we understand that each interaction is an opportunity to create value, we can approach our relationships with a sense of purpose and authenticity. Rather than allowing our actions to be led by fleeting emotions or assumptions, we can make deliberate choices that reflect who we are and the relationships we wish to cultivate.

The most successful relationships are those that are built on mutual trust, understanding, and respect. By "selling" ourselves authentically, we create a foundation for these qualities to thrive, enriching both our lives and the lives of those we connect with.

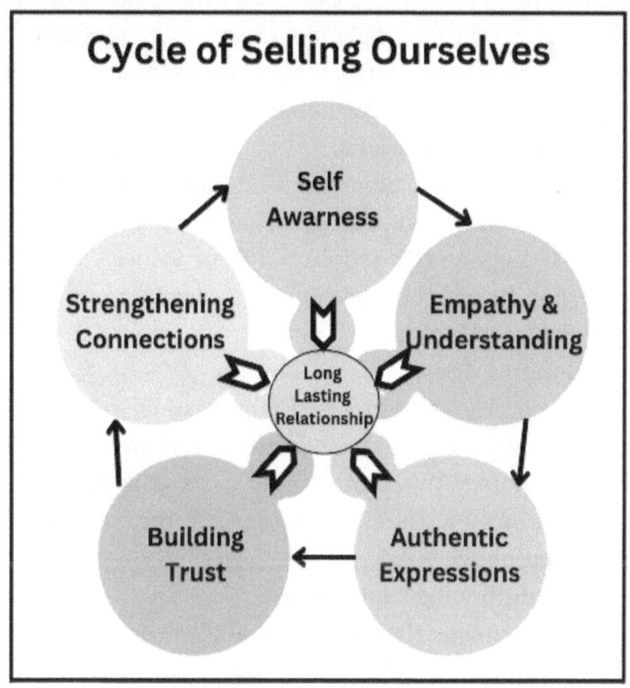

3. Cycle of Selling Ourselves

1. **Awareness of Self**

This first stage involves understanding our values, emotions, and motivations. Self-awareness allows us to bring authenticity into our relationships and recognize what we genuinely want to offer others. When we know our strengths and intentions, we can better express them in our interactions.

2. **Empathy and Understanding**

Empathy is key to connecting with others on a meaningful level. By placing ourselves in the other person's perspective, we gain insight into their needs, emotions, and expectations. This understanding helps us interact in a way that feels supportive and genuine to them.

3. Authentic Expression

Authenticity in communication builds trust. In this stage, we convey our thoughts, feelings, and intentions honestly, aligning our actions with our values. This open expression helps others see our true character and creates a foundation of honesty and respect.

4. Building Trust

Trust is the backbone of any lasting relationship. Consistency in our words and actions reinforces the trust we are building. When others see us as reliable and true to our promises, they feel secure in the relationship, strengthening the bond.

5. Strengthening Connections

As trust grows, relationships naturally deepen. This final stage is about nurturing the bonds created by showing continued interest, care, and support. With each interaction, the connection becomes more resilient, leading to a lasting, mutual sense of respect and loyalty.

Returning to Awareness of Self

Once a connection is strengthened, we return to self-awareness, reflecting on the growth from the relationship and adjusting our approach as needed. This self-reflection completes the cycle, making it a continuous journey of personal and relational development.

The Nature of Personal Relationships as Transactions

In our personal lives, we might not engage in financial transactions with the people we encounter, yet we still engage in a form of exchange. This exchange revolves around our presence, our time, our emotions, and the unique qualities that we bring into our relationships. When we interact with others—be it family, friends, or acquaintances—we are offering a piece of ourselves. This offering can be seen as a form of selling: we "sell" our authenticity, our care, and our companionship.

This exchange is not about commodifying relationships; rather, it is about understanding that every interaction carries value. Just as businesses seek to provide a superior product or service to retain their customers, we must cultivate qualities that enhance our personal relationships. This involves making others feel valued, respected, and understood. When we invest in our relationships by sharing our experiences, emotions, and insights, we create a bond that enriches both parties involved.

Selling ourselves in personal life stands apart from professional transactions, where products or services are exchanged and ownership changes hands. In personal relationships, "selling" ourselves doesn't involve giving something away that we lose; instead, it's about sharing our knowledge, experiences, and values in ways that enrich the lives of others without diminishing our own. When we offer our understanding, advice, or support, these qualities remain with us even as we share them, creating an ongoing flow of connection and influence. This approach fosters a unique type of relationship "transaction" that is additive and reciprocal, as each interaction builds a deeper, more resilient bond. This distinction emphasizes that personal relationships thrive not on material exchanges, but on intangible gifts—knowledge, empathy, and shared experiences—that deepen over time and continue to nurture both parties involved.

Enhancing Relationships Through Authenticity

To truly "sell" ourselves in personal relationships, we must first be authentic. Authenticity entails being genuine and true to oneself, which fosters trust and connection. When we present our true selves, we allow others to see and appreciate who we are at our core. This transparency is vital in establishing strong bonds with others.

For instance, consider a close friendship. The foundation of such a relationship often lies in the shared experiences and mutual understanding that develop over time. When friends are open about their feelings, thoughts, and vulnerabilities, they create a safe space for each other. This level of intimacy enhances the relationship, making it feel special and unique. In this way, authenticity acts as a currency in personal interactions, creating a deeper connection that is difficult to replicate.

In addition to authenticity, we "sell" support and compassion in our personal relationships. Every time we lend an ear to a friend in distress, provide comfort to a family member, or celebrate a loved one's achievements, we engage in an emotional exchange. This process strengthens the bond between individuals, fostering an environment of mutual support.

For example, consider a scenario where a friend is going through a tough time. By offering a listening ear, we validate their feelings and help them process their emotions. This simple act of compassion can significantly impact their well-being, enhancing the overall quality of the relationship. In this sense, we are "selling" our empathy and support, which are invaluable resources in maintaining healthy relationships.

Moreover, the practice of showing gratitude and appreciation can also be viewed as a form of emotional currency. Expressing gratitude not only acknowledges the efforts of others but also reinforces positive behaviours and deepens connections. When individuals feel appreciated, they are more likely to invest further in the relationship, creating a cycle of reciprocity that benefits both parties.

Building Trust: The Cornerstone of Meaningful Relationships

Trust is another vital component of selling ourselves in personal relationships. Like customers in a business transaction, individuals in personal life must feel secure and confident in the relationship. Trust is built over time through consistent actions and open communication. When we honour our commitments, respect boundaries, and communicate honestly, we lay the groundwork for trust to flourish.

For instance, in a romantic relationship, trust is essential for emotional intimacy. Partners must feel safe sharing their innermost thoughts and feelings without fear of judgment. By being reliable and supportive, individuals can cultivate an environment where trust thrives. In this way, we are "selling" a reliable and trustworthy presence, which is fundamental in creating lasting connections.

The Ripple Effect of Positive Relationships

The implications of our ability to "sell" ourselves in personal relationships extend beyond individual interactions; they create a ripple effect within our communities. As we cultivate meaningful connections with those around us, we contribute to a culture of support, kindness, and understanding.

When individuals prioritize relationships and invest in the emotional well-being of others, they foster a community where everyone feels valued. This environment encourages people to reach out, connect, and support one another, creating a stronger social fabric. In this sense, the act of "selling" ourselves in personal life has the potential to transform communities and promote a culture of empathy and compassion.

From Transaction to connection

The concept of customers transcends the confines of traditional commerce, inviting us to explore how we engage with one another in personal relationships. By recognizing that we "sell" ourselves—our authenticity, support, and trust—we can enhance our connections with others. These interactions, rooted in emotional exchanges and mutual respect, create special bonds that enrich our lives.

As we navigate our personal relationships, let us embrace the idea that every interaction carries value. By being authentic, compassionate, and trustworthy, we cultivate an environment where meaningful connections can flourish. Ultimately, the relationships we build not only enhance our own lives but also contribute to a more supportive and empathetic community. Thus, the act of "selling" ourselves becomes a powerful means of fostering connection and enriching the human experience.

CHAPTER FOUR

The Nature of Customer Relationships

Respect, Value, and Expectations

In traditional business discourse, the adage "the customer is always right" has prevailed, leading to the belief that customers should be treated as divine figures—akin to gods—in the marketplace. While this sentiment underscores the importance of customer satisfaction and loyalty, it raises essential questions about the appropriateness of such comparisons. Are customers, in their essence, comparable to deities? A closer examination reveals that while customers deserve respect and attention, the relationship should be rooted in mutual understanding and realistic expectations rather than idolatry.

The Reality of Customer Expectations

At the heart of the customer-business relationship lies the concept of value exchange. Customers pay for products and services with the expectation that they will receive quality, reliability, and value for their investment. In this context, it is important to acknowledge that customers do not merely demand good products; they seek an experience that justifies their expenditure.

In professional life, this relationship hinges on a delicate balance. As long as customers receive appropriate compensation for the value they provide, along with excellent support from the team, they can rightfully consider themselves customers. This mutual expectation defines the boundaries of the relationship. When a customer purchases a product or service, they enter into a contract—not merely transactional but based on an agreement of respect and quality. If this agreement falters—if the product fails to meet quality standards, or if the support falls short—the customer's perception of the relationship shifts. In such cases, customers may feel they are no longer being treated as valued patrons, leading to dissatisfaction and disengagement.

The Concept of Value in Professional Relationships

In a professional setting, the relationship with customers is built on a foundation of value. Organizations must strive to deliver not only products and services but also an overarching experience that embodies reliability and excellence. When customers feel their needs are met, their expectations are fulfilled, and their voices are heard, they are more likely to remain loyal.

To maintain this value, businesses must prioritize communication, quality control, and after-sales support. Regular feedback loops, where customers can voice their opinions and concerns, are crucial in building a sense of partnership. When customers see that their input influences decisions, they feel valued and respected, which enhances their overall experience.

Moreover, the concept of value in professional relationships extends beyond mere financial transactions. Customers also seek emotional and psychological reassurance that their choices are validated. They want to know that they made the right decision by choosing a particular brand or service. Therefore, businesses should aim to create a culture that recognizes the importance of emotional intelligence in customer interactions.

The Importance of Respect in Personal Relationships

Transitioning to personal relationships, the notion of respect takes centre stage. In this context, we often encounter individuals in our lives who can be classified as customers, albeit in a more abstract sense. These are the people we interact with daily—friends, family, acquaintances, and community members—whose relationships are defined by mutual respect and shared values.

The essence of maintaining personal customer relationships lies in the acknowledgment of dignity and worth. As long as respect is upheld and core values are shared, the relationship flourishes. Personal relationships thrive on open communication, empathy, and a willingness to listen. When individuals feel appreciated and understood, they are more likely to invest time and energy into nurturing the connection.

However, the moment respect diminishes—be it through neglect, misunderstandings, or disrespectful behaviour—the relationship risks breakdown. In personal life, relationships can be fragile, and any perceived slight can lead to significant emotional fallout. Thus, it is crucial to navigate these relationships with care, ensuring that both parties feel valued and respected.

Balancing Expectations and Reality

While it is important to emphasize the significance of respecting customers in both professional and personal contexts, it is equally vital to recognize the limitations of this comparison. The expectations that customers bring into relationships—whether in business or personal life—must be balanced with realistic outcomes.

In professional environments, customers should be aware that businesses operate within constraints, including budget limitations, resource availability, and market conditions. Likewise, in personal relationships, individuals must recognize that everyone is human and subject to mistakes and miscommunications. This awareness fosters an environment of understanding rather than entitlement, allowing relationships to adapt and evolve over time.

The Shift from Worship to Partnership

Rather than viewing customers as divine figures who demand unwavering service, a healthier perspective is to see them as partners in a collaborative relationship. This partnership is grounded in mutual respect, where both parties acknowledge their roles and responsibilities.

In professional settings, businesses should strive to empower customers by involving them in the decision-making process. By fostering a sense of ownership, customers feel more invested in the relationship, leading to increased loyalty and satisfaction. Conversely, customers should approach businesses as partners striving to deliver the best possible experience. This collaborative mindset helps to bridge the gap between expectation and reality, cultivating a more robust and enduring relationship.

Cultivating Respectful Partnerships

While the phrase "the customer is always right" has its merits, the notion of treating customers as gods can be misleading. A more nuanced understanding recognizes that customers are valuable partners who deserve respect and attention, but whose expectations must be managed realistically. In professional life, the relationship with customers is defined by a reciprocal exchange of value, where quality service and support are paramount. In personal relationships, maintaining respect and shared values is essential for fostering connections that endure over time.

Ultimately, by shifting our perspective from worshiping customers to partnering with them, we can cultivate relationships that are not only respectful but also enriching. This approach creates a culture of collaboration, understanding, and loyalty—ensuring that customers, whether in professional or personal contexts, feel valued for their contributions and presence in our lives. In this way, we not only enhance our relationships but also build a more compassionate and supportive community for all.

CHAPTER FIVE

The Art of Winning and Retaining Customers

A Pathway to Lasting Relationships

The process of acquiring a customer and retaining them for a lifetime is an essential, yet intricate, aspect of building successful relationships—whether professional or personal. It is an art that requires a deep understanding of human needs, attentive listening, and genuine engagement. To achieve lasting bonds, we must approach each customer interaction with a mindset that prioritizes understanding their current and future needs, as well as recognizing and supporting the values they hold dear.

Understanding Customer Needs: A Foundation for Trust

When engaging with customers, it is essential to remember that the initial approach sets the stage for the entire relationship. The priority should be to understand the customer's needs, requirements for today and tomorrow, and, most importantly, the values they seek in a partnership. This means stepping into their world, not with a script full of our own accolades and achievements, but with questions and solutions tailored to their aspirations.

Too often, we fall into the trap of leading conversations with what we bring to the table—our skills, our accomplishments, our story. However, this approach shifts the focus away from the customer and toward ourselves. Instead, we should aim to enter discussions ready to address their unique challenges, suggest ways to enhance their journey, and improve their outcomes. When we reach out with solutions that align with their vision, we allow them to see our capabilities not through self-promotion, but through the lens of partnership and mutual growth.

The Power of Listening and Empathy

A critical aspect of building strong relationships with customers is the art of listening. Both professional and personal customers value being heard and understood. When we take the time to listen to their stories, their achievements, and their current progress—even if we think we already know their background—we gain insights that might shift our perspective. This act of listening demonstrates respect and interest, and it often reveals nuances that may have been overlooked.

Listening attentively benefits both parties. For the customer, it reinforces the belief that their voice matters and their experiences are valued. For us, it provides a deeper understanding that informs how we can better serve them. This type of engagement creates a shared sense of partnership, where the customer feels seen and valued, paving the way for trust and openness to flourish.

The Benefits of Engaging Conversations

When we provide customers with the space and opportunity to share their requirements in detail, we uncover new possibilities for collaboration. This openness allows us to tailor our services or interactions to fit their needs precisely, which can lead to long-term relationships. For both professional and personal customers, the ability to communicate freely with us creates a safe and inviting environment. It opens the door for transparency, where expectations and visions are shared openly, fostering a deeper understanding.

As openness increases, so does reliability. Trust grows exponentially when customers know they can count on us to listen without judgment, respond thoughtfully, and follow through with solutions. This trust forms the backbone of enduring relationships, transforming transactional interactions into partnerships that are mutually beneficial.

Building Relationships That Blossom

When trust and open communication are established, the relationship blossoms. The benefits are mutual: customers receive personalized and reliable support, and we gain loyal partners who advocate for us and contribute to our growth. This synergy is the essence of customer engagement. It reflects a commitment to going beyond the superficial, showing that we prioritize the well-being and success of those we serve.

Furthermore, the practice of treating customers with empathy and respect reinforces our values. It teaches us patience, enhances our problem-solving abilities, and makes us more adept at handling complex situations. The more we practice this form of engagement, the more natural it becomes, transforming us into better communicators and, ultimately, more compassionate human beings.

Beyond Professional Boundaries: Personal Relationships

The principles of engaging, listening, and partnering with customers extend beyond the professional sphere into personal life. Just as professional customers value being heard and supported, so too do the individuals we interact with on a personal level. When we view friends, family, and acquaintances through the lens of respect and open communication, we strengthen those bonds and create relationships built on trust.

Personal customers, much like their professional counterparts, appreciate when we listen to their stories and achievements. By showing genuine interest and being open to hearing them out, even if we think we already know the details, we reinforce the connection. The result is a relationship that is both supportive and fulfilling, where mutual respect leads to deeper understanding and longer-lasting bonds.

The Transformation Through Respect and Openness

Ultimately, treating every customer—whether professional or personal—with respect and giving them space to share their experiences transforms our interactions. It encourages positive outcomes where relationships thrive and loyalty is earned. The key lies not in showcasing what we have achieved or what we are capable of but in showing that we care about their journey, their needs, and their success.

This approach fosters an environment where relationships are not just maintained but nurtured to grow and evolve over time. When we prioritize listening, demonstrate empathy, and engage in meaningful conversations, we become trusted partners in their journey. As a result, our reputation strengthens, and we become known as individuals or organizations that value connection, understanding, and shared progress.

Building a Legacy of Lasting Bonds

To win a customer and retain them for life is to master the art of thoughtful interaction. It requires us to approach each relationship with a willingness to understand, listen, and engage. By doing so, we create an atmosphere of trust and reliability where customers feel free to communicate openly. This foundation supports the growth of relationships that last beyond initial interactions and leads to mutual success.

Adopting this mindset in all areas of life helps us cultivate a reputation of respect, making us better professionals, friends, and community members. Through our commitment to open communication and empathy, we not only retain customers but also enrich our own experiences and personal growth. This journey shapes us into individuals who bring value and love into every relationship, ensuring that each connection we make is meaningful and enduring.

Quadrant for Customer Winning and Retention Strategies

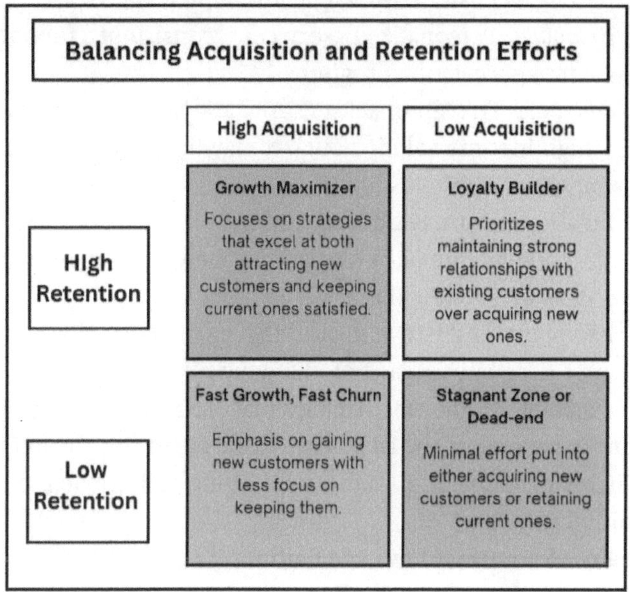

4. Balancing Acquisition and Retention Efforts

High Retention, High Acquisition

Description: This quadrant focuses on strategies that excel at both attracting new customers and keeping current ones satisfied.

Examples: Exceptional customer experience, loyalty programs, ongoing value delivery, regular communication, and personalization.

Outcome: These strategies foster brand loyalty while bringing in a steady influx of new customers, creating a sustainable, growth-oriented business model.

High Retention, Low Acquisition

Description: Prioritizes maintaining strong relationships with existing customers over acquiring new ones.

Examples: Personalized services, consistent support, customer appreciation programs.

Outcome: This approach ensures a loyal customer base with high lifetime value, though it may limit growth if new customer acquisition is too low.

Low Retention, High Acquisition

Description: Emphasis on gaining new customers with less focus on keeping them.

Examples: Aggressive marketing campaigns, discounts for first-time buyers, lack of follow-up.

Outcome: While this strategy may lead to quick growth in new customers, the lack of retention efforts may result in a high churn rate and a more challenging path to long-term profitability.

Low Retention, Low Acquisition

Description: Minimal effort put into either acquiring new customers or retaining current ones.

Examples: Limited engagement, lack of customer-focused strategies, or inconsistency in service quality.

Outcome: This approach leads to stagnation or decline, as it neither attracts new customers nor nurtures relationships with existing ones, risking a loss in market share.

CHAPTER SIX

The Ethical Bedrock of Customer Retention

The Principle of Non-Disclosure

In both personal and professional relationships, the trust built between individuals and their 'customers'—those they interact with—is a pillar that holds the relationship together. One of the most fundamental ethical principles in maintaining and nurturing this trust is the commitment to non-disclosure. This principle refers to the responsibility of keeping any personal or professional information shared in confidence strictly private. Upholding this principle is not just a practice; it is a foundational ethic that signifies respect, loyalty, and integrity. It forms the bedrock upon which lasting relationships are built and retained.

The Role of Trust in Customer Retention

Trust is the cornerstone of all meaningful relationships, and maintaining that trust requires unwavering commitment. Customers, whether they are colleagues, friends, family members, or professional clients, seek a safe space where they can express themselves freely without fear of their words being shared inappropriately or without consent. When we actively uphold non-disclosure, we reinforce that sense of safety and establish ourselves as trustworthy partners or confidants.

This commitment to confidentiality demonstrates that we value the relationship enough to protect it. It communicates that the relationship itself is more important than any personal gain that might come from sharing what we know. For example, in professional settings, an employee might share sensitive feedback or personal challenges with a supervisor or peer. The expectation is that such disclosures remain private, ensuring that the workplace remains a safe and respectful environment. If we compromise this trust, the repercussions can be damaging and irreversible.

Openness and Its Responsibilities

When a relationship evolves and deepens, so too does the openness between the parties involved. Customers—whether in business or in life—begin to share insights, stories, and concerns that they may have never shared with anyone else. This openness is a sign of trust, and it comes with the inherent responsibility of safeguarding what has been disclosed.

The information shared during these moments often has significant personal value to the individual sharing it. In personal life, for instance, a friend might confide something sensitive, trusting that their words will be held in the strictest confidence. Even if a spouse or close relative inquire about that conversation, maintaining the ethics of non-disclosure means choosing to honour the friend's trust over satisfying the curiosity of another. While it is true that spouses share many aspects of their lives and have an intimate understanding, the principle of confidentiality

lies in the responsibility of the person entrusted with the information—not in an assumed obligation to share everything they know.

In professional life, the same rule applies. For example, if a head of department (HOD) discusses challenges with their subordinates or vice versa, it is our duty to keep those conversations private. To disclose such details, even casually, is a breach of trust that can disrupt relationships and damage the culture of the organization. Upholding non-disclosure ensures that people feel safe discussing their concerns, knowing that their words will not resurface in unwanted ways.

Non-Disclosure: A Lifelong Commitment

Non-disclosure is not a temporary agreement; it is a lifelong commitment. The conversations we engage in, whether in a personal or professional capacity, carry an implicit promise of discretion. This is especially important in situations where sensitive or confidential information is shared. The understanding is that what is shared with us remains with us, not just during the duration of the relationship but indefinitely.

When we commit to upholding the principle of non-disclosure, we create a culture of trust that paves the way for deeper, more meaningful relationships. People are more inclined to open up when they know that their thoughts, opinions, and personal information will be respected and protected. This openness can lead to improved communication, stronger bonds, and more productive collaborations. However, breaking this principle can lead to fractured relationships and a significant loss of trust, which is difficult to rebuild.

The Power of Trust in Retention and Success

Customer retention, whether in personal or professional settings, is highly influenced by the trust that is built through respecting confidentiality. When customers or individuals know that their information is safe with us, they are more likely to continue engaging and investing in the relationship. This leads to stronger partnerships, more effective teamwork, and deeper personal connections.

Non-disclosure is not just about withholding information; it is about demonstrating that we value the people in our lives enough to protect their stories. It is an ethical practice that aligns with loyalty, reliability, and a deep sense of respect. These qualities are not just desirable but essential for the success and sustainability of relationships.

Upholding this fundamental principle ultimately leads to a progressive path where customer relationships not only survive but thrive. When we protect the confidence placed in us, we reinforce our reputation as trustworthy individuals, capable of maintaining and nurturing relationships over a lifetime. This commitment to non-disclosure is what transforms ordinary relationships into bonds of mutual respect and loyalty, laying the groundwork for enduring success.

Building a Legacy of Trust

The practice of non-disclosure is an ethical imperative that shapes how we interact with the people who trust us with their thoughts, experiences, and challenges. Whether in professional or personal contexts, maintaining the confidentiality of what is shared with us is key to building trust, fostering openness, and ensuring the longevity of relationships. By adhering to this principle, we solidify the bonds that hold our relationships together and set a standard for how we wish to be treated in return.

The value of this commitment cannot be overstated. It is the difference between fleeting interactions and relationships that last a lifetime. When we choose to respect the confidence placed in us, we are not just preserving trust; we are building a legacy of integrity that defines who we are as individuals.

CHAPTER SEVEN

The Power of Customer Retention

Pathways to Growth and Success

Customer retention is not merely a business strategy; it is a comprehensive approach that enriches relationships and fosters growth in both personal and professional life. The act of retaining customers—whether they are colleagues, friends, or clients—opens the door to a myriad of possibilities. By nurturing these relationships and creating meaningful connections, we build a network that sustains and propels our success in ways that often surpass conventional efforts.

Personal Growth Through Impactful Relationships

In personal life, customer retention goes beyond maintaining simple connections. It's about creating a lasting impact on the lives of those we meet. When we influence others positively, they become more inclined to introduce us to other good people within their circles. This process of expanding one's network has immense potential; it brings unexpected opportunities, insights, and support that can be invaluable at different points in life. The beauty of this growth lies in its unpredictability—we often do not know who will become an important contact or how they may help us down the line. The bonds we form today can become the bridges that connect us to new experiences and people who enrich our journey.

For example, a friend whom we have supported through difficult times may later introduce us to someone with shared interests or complementary skills. This new connection could lead to collaborative projects, professional opportunities, or even lifelong friendships. Personal growth through customer retention isn't about immediate gains; it's about fostering relationships that open doors to continued learning, collaboration, and shared success.

Professional Success Through Comprehensive Engagement

In the realm of professional life, the benefits of focusing on customer retention are even more pronounced. By dedicating our attention to both internal and external customers, we set the stage for outstanding success. Internal customers—such as team members, colleagues, and support staff—are the backbone of any business or professional endeavour. When they feel valued and supported, their loyalty and commitment deepen, which translates to higher productivity and a more harmonious work environment. Internal customers often become close associates who amplify our influence within an organization and champion our ideas and projects.

External customers, on the other hand, are those who purchase our products or services or engage with us from outside the immediate circle of our professional sphere. When we prioritize their satisfaction and view them as partners, they become more than one-time clients; they become advocates. Their recommendations and word-of-mouth endorsements extend our reach to their friends, colleagues, and professional networks. This type of organic growth has the power to elevate our reputation, making us a preferred choice in our field.

Customers as Indirect Partners in Growth

A fundamental shift occurs when we treat customers—whether internal or external—as partners in our journey. By investing in their needs, listening to their feedback, and providing value, we inspire loyalty that transforms our relationship from transactional to cooperative. Customers, in turn, contribute indirectly to our growth. They become invested in our success because it aligns with their satisfaction and well-being. This partnership approach means that customers will not only continue to engage with us but will also work on our behalf by spreading positive impressions and encouraging others to connect with us.

In business, this kind of relationship fosters financial growth. When customers feel valued, they remain loyal, reducing the cost and effort of acquiring new customers. Their advocacy brings in new business organically, without the need for extensive marketing efforts. Our consistent, customer-centric approach becomes its own form of unique marketing—a natural extension of our brand that attracts others through the positive experiences of those we have already served.

Financial and Business Growth Through Retention

The financial success of any business hinges on its ability to retain customers. Retaining a satisfied customer is significantly more cost-effective than acquiring a new one, and loyal customers often spend more over time. They also tend to refer others, creating a cycle of growth that builds on itself. By focusing on customer retention, businesses can reduce marketing costs and increase their return on investment. Moreover, the consistent revenue from returning customers provides stability, allowing for strategic growth and innovation.

What sets customer retention apart as a unique form of marketing is the authenticity it carries. Traditional marketing efforts often aim to highlight the benefits of a product or service, but when customers speak on our behalf, their recommendations come with credibility and trust. This trust translates into higher conversion rates, as potential customers are more likely to be influenced by personal stories and referrals than by advertising alone.

The Unique Approach: A Strategy of Connection

Approaching customer relationships with a mindset of genuine partnership is, in itself, a marketing strategy. When we prioritize the needs of our customers and ensure that our interactions are meaningful, we create experiences that leave a lasting impression. This type of customer engagement emphasizes trust, respect, and value. It becomes the foundation upon which loyalty is built, encouraging customers to become ambassadors for our brand or personal endeavours.

By treating every interaction as an opportunity to strengthen the relationship, we harness the potential for long-term growth. This is true not only in business but in every facet of life. Our approach becomes an emblem of who we are and what we stand for—a commitment to integrity, excellence, and the well-being of those we serve.

The Transformative Power of Retention

Customer retention is more than a strategy; it is a transformative practice that enriches both personal and professional life. By creating impact and fostering trust, we pave the way for growth that extends beyond immediate gains. In personal life, this approach broadens our network and enhances our experiences through the relationships we cultivate. In professional life, it establishes a foundation for sustained success through partnerships that promote loyalty, advocacy, and financial stability.

When we view customers as partners, we invite them to share in our journey. This perspective not only benefits our growth but also strengthens the fabric of our interactions, making them more fulfilling and resilient. The results are profound—relationships that last, trust that endures, and a legacy of connection that propels us forward.

Cycle of Customer Retention

Customer retention is more than just maintaining a steady client base; it is an intricate cycle of nurturing relationships that fuel both personal and business growth. At its core, retention embodies empathy, trust, and mutual value, transforming interactions into long-term partnerships that foster loyalty and advocacy. In today's competitive landscape, businesses that prioritize building and sustaining meaningful relationships stand out as beacons of reliability and trust. This focus on retaining customers, rather than solely acquiring new ones, leads to sustainable growth, reduced marketing costs, and a strong network of customer advocates. Understanding and embracing the cycle of customer retention is not only strategic but essential for creating lasting success and resilience in any endeavour. These following eight points are important and form an unavoidable cycle of customer retention.

1. ***Empathy and Connection*** → Build meaningful relationships through genuine understanding.

2. ***Personalized Engagement*** → Tailor interactions to address specific customer needs.

3. ***Trust and Loyalty*** → Foster trust through consistent, value-driven communication.

4. ***Advocacy and Word-of-Mouth*** → Encourage satisfied customers to share positive experiences.

5. ***Sustainable Growth*** → Benefit from cost-effective growth and reduced acquisition efforts.

6. ***Feedback and Improvement*** → Collect and act on feedback to enhance future interactions.

7. ***Strengthened Relationships*** → Deepen connections that support long-term success.

8. **Mutual Benefit** → Reinforce partnerships where both parties thrive.

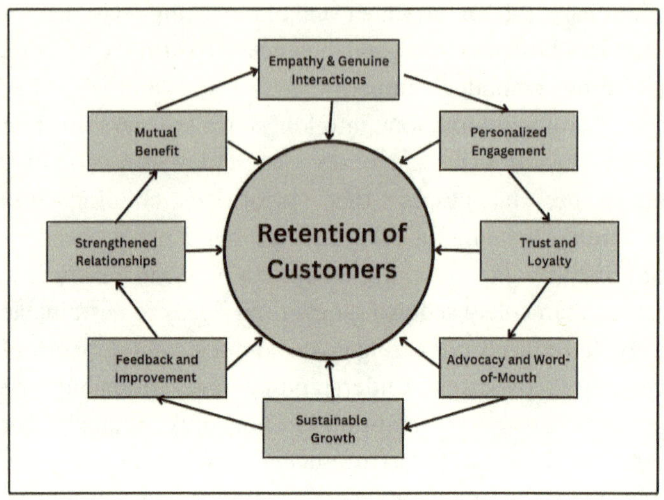

5. Customer Retention Cycle

1. Empathy and Connection

Empathy is the foundation of lasting relationships. In customer retention, empathy means going beyond addressing immediate needs and showing a genuine interest in the customer's experience. By understanding their emotions and perspectives, businesses build a connection that resonates with customers on a personal level. This connection not only resolves issues but also makes customers feel valued and understood, which deepens their loyalty. For example, customer service representatives who actively listen and respond with compassion can turn a negative experience into a positive one, reinforcing the bond with the customer.

2. Personalized Engagement

Customers appreciate interactions that are tailored to their unique preferences and needs. Personalized engagement can include remembering past purchases, customizing product recommendations, or offering solutions based on a customer's history. This level of attention shows that the business sees the customer as an individual rather than just a number. Such engagement strengthens the relationship by demonstrating that the business is committed to meeting the customer's specific needs, enhancing their overall satisfaction and loyalty.

3. Trust and Loyalty

Trust is the bedrock of customer retention. It is built through consistent and transparent communication, reliable service, and a commitment to fulfilling promises. Loyalty develops when customers know they can depend on a business to act with integrity. This trust is fostered over time through actions that consistently align with the business's values. For instance, providing prompt solutions to problems, admitting mistakes, and offering honest timelines for resolutions create a sense of security that encourages customers to return and stay loyal.

4. Advocacy and Word-of-Mouth

Satisfied customers naturally become advocates. They share their positive experiences with friends, family, and colleagues, contributing to organic growth. Word-of-mouth marketing is one of the most powerful forms of advertising because it comes with built-in trust. When customers speak positively about a business, it carries more weight than traditional marketing efforts. Businesses that prioritize retention reap the benefits of this type of advocacy, as customers willingly promote their services or products, expanding their reach and attracting new clients without additional marketing expenses.

5. Sustainable Growth

Focusing on customer retention leads to sustainable growth. The cost of retaining existing customers is significantly lower than acquiring new ones, which helps businesses maintain stable revenue streams. Loyal customers are more likely to make repeat purchases and spend more over time, contributing to financial stability. This growth is more predictable and consistent, enabling the business to allocate resources more effectively and plan for long-term development. A customer base that feels valued continues to support the business, allowing for incremental and steady expansion.

6. Feedback and Improvement

Customer retention isn't static; it thrives on continuous improvement. By seeking feedback from existing customers, businesses can identify areas for enhancement and innovate their offerings. This feedback loop is vital for maintaining relevance and adapting to changing customer needs. Customers who feel heard are more inclined to stay loyal because they see their input leading to real changes. Regularly implementing customer-driven improvements ensures that the business stays aligned with expectations, reinforcing customer satisfaction and loyalty.

7. Strengthened Relationships

Customer retention is ultimately about building relationships that withstand challenges. Strong relationships are resilient and enable businesses to navigate difficult times with their customers by their side. These relationships are built on repeated positive interactions, reliability, and a shared history of mutual respect. Customers who have been with a business through various experiences are more understanding and forgiving when occasional issues arise. This loyalty helps the business weather tough periods and maintain a loyal customer base that continues to engage even during fluctuations in the market.

8. Mutual Benefit

Retention strategies that prioritize the customer create a dynamic of mutual benefit. When customers feel appreciated and supported, they invest back into the relationship, either through continued patronage or by recommending the business to others. This mutual loyalty leads to a cycle where both parties gain: customers enjoy consistent value and positive experiences, and businesses benefit from sustained revenue and a strong reputation. Viewing retention as a partnership rather than a transactional interaction ensures that both the business and the customer thrive.

CHAPTER EIGHT

The Art of Accepting Feedback

The Importance of Customer Feedback: A Path to Growth

Customer feedback is a cornerstone for personal and professional growth. It provides invaluable insights into how we are perceived and helps identify areas for improvement. Whether dealing with customers in a personal or professional capacity, embracing feedback is crucial for fostering strong, lasting relationships.

Navigating Personal Attachments and Feedback

In our personal lives, our "customers" are the people closest to us—family, friends, and acquaintances with whom we share deep emotional bonds. These non-commercial relationships are unique because they are built on love, trust, and shared experiences. However, these attachments can sometimes create barriers to honest feedback. Emotional closeness may lead us to unintentionally discourage open communication, as we may fear criticism or feel protective of our interactions.

Understanding the nature of these relationships and setting aside emotional barriers is essential. When we allow our close ones to provide feedback freely, without fear of judgment or negative reactions, we invite growth into our relationships. Feedback on our behaviours, actions, and habits can help us become more self-aware and foster smoother interactions. The willingness to receive and act on feedback shows maturity and respect for those who care about us, ultimately strengthening bonds over time.

The Professional Sphere: Feedback as a Key to Success

In the professional world, the importance of customer feedback cannot be overstated. External customers—clients who use our products or services—are essential to a business's success. While building strong relationships with them can lead to loyalty and mutual benefit, there must be boundaries to maintain a professional atmosphere that prioritizes constructive criticism. If a business discourages open feedback from its customers, it risks stagnation and eventual decline. Regardless of how close a company becomes with its clients, it must never take the relationship for granted. The moment customers feel unable to express their concerns or share feedback, they will begin seeking alternatives.

Equally important are internal customers, such as team members, vendors, and other associates. They play a pivotal role in the operational success of an organization. A common pitfall is for leaders to adopt a mindset of authority, believing that paying salaries justifies dismissing feedback. This approach can drive away talented individuals and stifle growth. Smart, driven people prefer environments where their voices are heard and valued. By fostering an atmosphere where feedback is welcomed from all levels of an organization, a company can tap into a wealth of insights that improve performance and innovation.

Embracing Feedback Without Ego

One of the greatest challenges in accepting feedback is separating it from personal ego. Whether in personal or professional settings, it is easy to feel defensive when faced with criticism. However, true growth comes from listening without interruption, analysing the feedback thoughtfully, and taking actionable steps to improve. The process involves humility and a willingness to learn. When feedback is offered, our response should not be immediate justification or defensive but attentive listening.

Acting on feedback should be viewed as an opportunity for transformation. Once changes have been made, it is essential to follow up with the person who provided the feedback, acknowledging their input and expressing gratitude. This gesture not only shows that their opinions are valued but also reinforces trust and respect.

The Benefits of Open Feedback

The benefits of embracing feedback are multifaceted. In personal life, creating a space where feedback is welcomed helps us grow as individuals and strengthens our relationships. People appreciate being heard and knowing that their opinions contribute to positive change. In professional life, an environment where feedback is integral to the culture fosters innovation, efficiency, and teamwork. Customers who feel their voices matter are more likely to remain loyal, promoting long-term success.

Feedback should be seen not as criticism but as a tool for enhancement. It builds resilience, improves communication, and helps create a culture of continuous improvement. When we listen wholeheartedly and respond positively to feedback, we not only build stronger relationships but also lay the foundation for sustained personal and professional growth.

The following quadrant provides valuable insight into the importance and necessity of feedback.

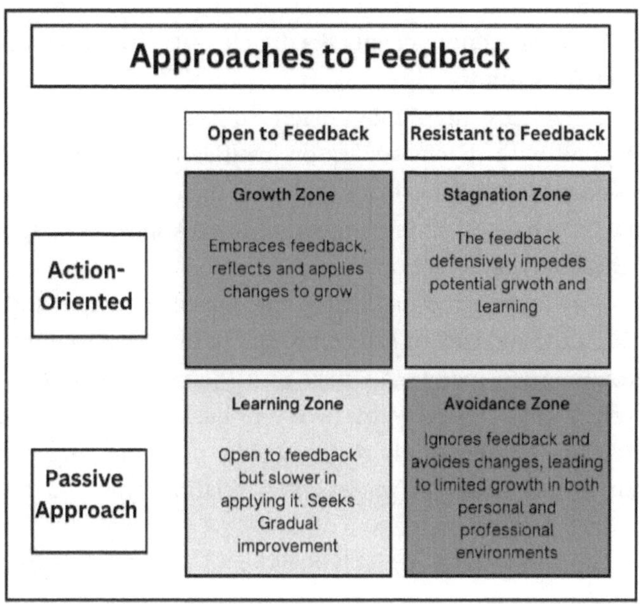

6. Approaches to Feedback Quadrant

Avoidance Zone: Ignores Feedback and Avoids Change

Individuals in this quadrant tend to disregard feedback, either out of fear, denial, or unwillingness to accept criticism. They are often resistant to change and may view feedback as an attack rather than an opportunity for improvement.

By ignoring feedback, they limit their own growth in both personal and professional contexts. This approach can lead to stagnant development, as they miss valuable insights and opportunities to improve skills, relationships, and overall performance. Over time, this attitude may hinder progress, reduce credibility, and limit career advancements.

Reactive Zone: Accepts Feedback, but with Resistance or Defensiveness

Individuals here may listen to feedback but often respond with defensiveness or justifications. They might acknowledge the feedback but feel uncomfortable about making changes or implementing suggestions, leading to partial or delayed action.

This approach can yield some improvement, but the resistance and lack of full commitment may lead to limited growth. Such individuals may find themselves stuck in a cycle of "one step forward, two steps back," achieving some progress but never fully realizing their potential. This zone can create strain in professional relationships and may signal a lack of openness to others.

Learning Zone: Actively Seeks and Accepts Feedback with Openness

People in the Learning Zone actively seek constructive feedback and show genuine interest in self-improvement. They approach feedback with an open mind, a willingness to learn, and a positive attitude toward making adjustments.

Embracing feedback openly helps them experience steady growth, both personally and professionally. They not only improve in their current roles but also build stronger, more resilient relationships. This approach fosters continuous learning, enhances adaptability, and positions them as motivated and proactive contributors to their environment.

Growth Zone: Embraces Feedback and Proactively Implements Change

In the Growth Zone, individuals embrace feedback with enthusiasm and proactively make changes based on it. They view feedback as essential to their development and are quick to adapt, experimenting with new methods and approaches to maximize their potential.

This approach leads to accelerated growth and transformation, as they consistently evolve through the feedback process. Such individuals often achieve excellence in their roles and inspire others by setting a positive example of adaptability and commitment to personal and professional growth. The Growth Zone represents the ideal attitude for leaders and high achievers, as it combines openness with a strong drive for continuous improvement.

CHAPTER NINE

Keeping Customers Updated

A Key to Sustaining Engagement

One of the essential practices in nurturing customer relationships—whether in personal or professional contexts—is consistently updating them on progress. By sharing updates on progress and outlining general plans for implementation, we can maintain interest, build trust, and ensure customers are aligned with our vision. This practice does not entail revealing every detail of our strategy but rather providing a broad overview that fosters understanding and keeps our customers prepared to support us or utilize our services when the need arises.

Progress Updates in Personal Life

In personal life, customers encompass our family, friends, and close acquaintances. Keeping these internal customers informed about our progress in various areas, whether related to personal goals, projects, or life transitions, fosters a sense of connection and support.

Family and friends often play the role of cheerleaders, rooting for our success and offering encouragement. By updating them, we invite their input, which can be invaluable. These individuals bring perspectives that may highlight potential pitfalls or advantages we might have overlooked. While we might not always agree with their assessments, their insights often contain nuggets of wisdom that help refine our approach and guide us toward achieving our vision.

Moreover, keeping friends and family informed has practical benefits. When they are aware of our ongoing efforts, they may connect us with opportunities or resources that align with our goals. For instance, a friend who knows about a business project may recommend a valuable contact, or a family member aware of our career aspirations might share information about an upcoming opportunity. This network of support can make a substantial difference in navigating the path toward success.

Progress Updates in Professional Life

In a professional context, keeping external customers informed about progress and future plans is vital for maintaining strong, proactive relationships. Clients and business partners appreciate transparency, as it reassures them that their trust is well-placed and that their investment or interest in our services is respected. Regular updates about the general direction of a project or business growth can create anticipation and position us as a reliable partner in their future plans.

Updating customers about progress does not mean disclosing every detail of our action plans. Instead, it involves sharing strategic information that highlights our vision and progress milestones. This approach helps manage customer expectations and builds confidence in our capability to meet future needs. When customers are kept in the loop, they are more likely to plan their activities around our timeline and support us by availing themselves of our services or products when ready.

The Balance of Transparency and Discretion

While it is important to keep customers updated, there is an equally crucial balance to maintain: ensuring that updates are meaningful without revealing sensitive details. Sharing too much information can lead to misunderstandings or create unnecessary vulnerabilities. By providing a high-level overview that communicates progress without delving into the intricacies of an action plan, we can safeguard our interests while still engaging our customers effectively.

This principle holds true in both personal and professional settings. In personal life, sharing every detail of our plans can sometimes lead to over-analysis or unsolicited advice that may not be productive. In a professional setting, disclosing too much can expose strategic moves to competitors or create unrealistic expectations among customers.

The Benefits of Updating Customers

Keeping customers posted about progress has several tangible benefits. In personal life, it strengthens relationships and nurtures a culture of mutual support. Friends and family who are updated about our efforts often become invested in our journey, celebrating our milestones and lending support when needed. This practice also helps reinforce bonds by making others feel valued and included in our lives.

In the professional realm, regular updates ensure that customers remain engaged and ready to support our ventures. Customers who feel informed are more likely to stay loyal and advocate for our business. This can lead to word-of-mouth referrals, partnerships, and an overall boost in reputation. Furthermore, when customers are aware of our progress, they can provide timely feedback or assistance that aligns with their experiences and expertise, contributing to the shared success of both parties.

The Power of Transparent Communication

In summary, maintaining open lines of communication with customers and keeping them updated on progress is an essential practice that benefits both personal and professional relationships. By providing relevant updates that build trust and engagement, we create a supportive environment where customers feel included and valued. This practice enhances our ability to reach our goals and ensures that when the time comes for our products or services to be available, customers are prepared to embrace them. The balance lies in sharing enough to foster interest and trust, without disclosing every detail. Ultimately, this approach strengthens relationships, creates mutual respect, and propels growth in all aspects of life.

CHAPTER TEN

Balancing Boundaries Friends vs. Customers

Drawing the Line Between Friends and Customers

The phrase "All friends can be customers, but customers cannot be friends" holds significant wisdom and serves as a crucial reminder in both personal and professional life. The ability to distinguish between friends and customers and to maintain appropriate boundaries with each is essential for fostering healthy and sustainable relationships. Often, we may overlook or blur these distinctions, but doing so can lead to challenges that may hinder both personal and professional growth.

Personal Relationships: Friends as Customers

In personal life, it is common to treat friends, family, and acquaintances as customers. We extend kindness, provide support, and strive to nurture relationships with those close to us. However, it is equally important to recognize that even in these intimate circles, there are boundaries that must be respected. Every individual has limitations, and understanding where to draw the line is essential to maintaining respect and balance within relationships.

For example, while it is natural to provide help and extend support to friends and family, recognizing when to step back and not overextend ourselves ensures that the relationship remains healthy. By treating personal relationships with the same care as a professional one but with emotional intelligence, we avoid misunderstandings and foster an environment where everyone's boundaries are respected. Practicing and implementing these principles in day-to-day interactions can lead to long-term benefits and the attainment of personal growth and strong, enduring bonds.

Professional Relationships: Customers and Boundaries

In the professional world, the dynamic between customers and providers is rooted in purpose, reason, and the exchange of value. Whether dealing with internal or external customers, these relationships are often defined by financial transactions, contracts, or mutual benefits that involve expectations and deliverables. Therefore, while it may be tempting to develop friendships with customers or clients, it is crucial to maintain a professional distance. This ensures that ethical standards are upheld and that interactions remain courteous and clear.

The reason for this boundary is simple: professional relationships, whether with team members, vendors, or clients, have an underlying structure that revolves around objectives and compensation. Any deviation into friendship can blur lines and create conflicts of interest or misunderstandings. For example, an overly familiar relationship with a client could lead to challenges when discussing difficult issues such as contract terms, pricing, or performance expectations. Such closeness could compromise decision-making, leading to unfavourable outcomes for both the individual and the organization.

Ethical and Courteous Reasons for Boundaries

Maintaining the appropriate distance with customers, whether internal or external, is also important for ethical and professional reasons. Customers should be kept close enough to ensure trust and open communication, but far enough to preserve professionalism and avoid potential conflicts. Striking this balance is key to upholding an organization's reputation and ensuring personal integrity.

Failing to recognize these boundaries can result in consequences that affect not only the individual but the entire organization. For example, when personal friendships influence business decisions, it can lead to biases, unfair practices, or even ethical breaches. By keeping professional relationships clear-cut and guided by mutual respect rather than personal attachment, individuals can maintain credibility and foster an environment of trust.

The Benefits of Understanding Boundaries

Recognizing the fine line between friends and customers and adhering to it can have significant benefits. In personal life, it helps in nurturing relationships that are respectful and long-lasting, where each party understands and honours the limits of their interactions. In professional settings, maintaining the proper boundaries ensures that business relationships are built on trust, fairness, and transparency.

Ultimately, being mindful of these distinctions empowers individuals to navigate their personal and professional lives with greater clarity and integrity. It fosters relationships that are beneficial, supportive, and sustainable, allowing for growth and success without the complications that blurred boundaries might bring.

CHAPTER ELEVEN

The Balance of Genuine Customer Relationships

The Dynamics of Genuine Customer Relationships

Understanding the nature of customer relationships, whether personal or professional, is fundamental to maintaining meaningful and sustainable connections. Customers are customers as long as they reciprocate with value—this may come in the form of rewards, appreciation, financial compensation, or other relevant forms of acknowledgment. When this reciprocation ceases, it becomes essential to address the situation and determine whether the relationship can be salvaged or if it has reached a critical turning point.

Evaluating the Situation

Relationships evolve over time, often built on trust, shared values, and mutual benefit. When a customer stops reciprocating, the first step is to assess the underlying reasons. It's important to approach the situation with empathy and a willingness to understand their perspective. Are they facing personal challenges that prevent them from responding in kind? Are there obstacles they cannot share, or is there a deeper issue that has affected their ability to engage?

Reaching out to check on the customer's well-being demonstrates that the relationship is valued beyond mere transactions. This effort can reveal whether the lack of reciprocation is due to temporary challenges or whether it reflects a fundamental aspect of the customer's nature. If the latter is true—if it becomes clear that their intention was never genuine—it is important to acknowledge the reality of the situation without regret. Misjudgements happen, and recognizing them provides an opportunity to adjust expectations and improve discernment in future interactions.

Letting Go and Moving Forward

Understanding when to let go is an essential part of maintaining balance and well-being, especially in relationships where intentions are not genuine. When it becomes clear that a customer's intentions do not align with fairness or mutual respect, it is necessary to accept that the energy and effort spent may not lead to positive outcomes. This realization, while challenging, offers a unique opportunity to reflect and grow. Acknowledging this reality empowers individuals to reclaim their focus and avoid wasting further resources on unproductive interactions.

The act of moving on should be seen not as a failure, but as an important learning moment. Each such encounter provides valuable insight into better assessing future relationships and interactions. It fosters the development of intuition and judgment, strengthening one's ability to identify the signs of a reliable partnership versus a deceptive one. By adopting this perspective, one can approach future relationships with heightened awareness and confidence.

Ultimately, letting go and moving forward is about prioritizing self-growth and emotional health. It underscores the importance of not allowing past disappointments to overshadow future opportunities. Instead, use these experiences as stepping stones, enriching personal and professional life with newfound clarity and resilience. This mindset ensures that energy is channelled into relationships that inspire growth, trust, and mutual benefit, paving the way for a more positive, forward-focused journey.

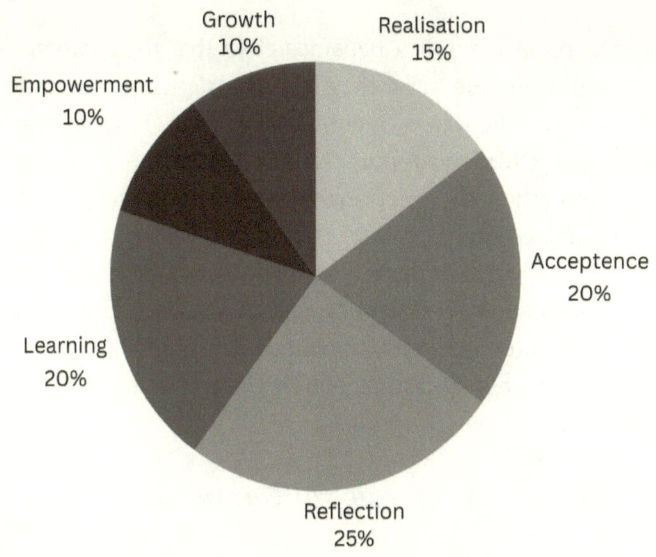

7. Process of Letting Go and Moving Forward

Realization: Recognizing when relationships are not aligned with fairness or respect.

Acceptance: Coming to terms with the need to let go.

Reflection: Taking time to think about the experience and its implications.

Learning: Gaining insights that help assess future interactions.

Empowerment: Feeling strengthened and motivated to focus on healthier relationships.

Growth: Prioritizing emotional health and personal development.

Supporting Genuine Customers

On the other hand, if it becomes clear that the customer's intentions are good and they are experiencing difficulties that prevent them from reciprocating, a different approach is needed. Offering support during these challenging times can strengthen the relationship and demonstrate loyalty and compassion. Genuine customers, those who have shown consistent integrity and appreciation in the past, are more likely to remember acts of kindness and return the favor when circumstances improve. This loyalty is the foundation of long-lasting connections that benefit both parties.

Personal vs. Professional Contexts

In personal life, genuine individuals often hesitate to reach out during their times of struggle. They may withdraw to avoid burdening others or to protect their loved ones from worry. Recognizing this pattern can help us be more proactive in supporting friends and family, even when they don't ask for it. The bond becomes more resilient when we show that we care without being prompted, fostering deeper trust and understanding.

In professional life, the behaviour of genuine customers may differ slightly. When faced with difficulties, they are more likely to communicate openly, requesting patience or explaining their situation. These customers value the relationship and will take steps to ensure that trust is maintained, even if they need more time. When they do this, it's an indicator that they view the partnership as mutually beneficial and worth preserving. Supporting them during these periods can result in continued loyalty and long-term success for both parties.

The Long-Term Perspective

Maintaining a balance between empathy and discernment is essential for nurturing customer relationships that are both fulfilling and productive. While it is important to show kindness and offer support, it is equally important to recognize when a relationship is no longer beneficial and take the necessary steps to protect one's own interests. Genuine relationships are characterized by reciprocal loyalty and trust, and by prioritizing these qualities, we can ensure that our interactions are meaningful and enduring.

The process of understanding, evaluating, and sometimes letting go of certain relationships helps us cultivate stronger, more authentic connections. Whether in personal or professional settings, learning to navigate these dynamics ensures that we build a network that not only supports us but also contributes to our growth and success.

CHAPTER TWELVE

Understanding and Navigating Different Kinds of Customers

In our interactions, whether in professional or personal settings, we encounter various types of customers, each characterized by distinct behaviours and expectations. Identifying and understanding these types allows us to manage relationships more effectively and maintain our well-being and success. Broadly, customers can be classified into two main kinds of categories: Genuine Customers and Toxic Customers. Each category also has sub-kinds that further define their characteristics and how they can be managed.

1. Genuine Customers

Genuine customers are those who are honest and committed. They uphold their promises and terms, and dealing with them often leads to positive experiences and long-term relationships. However, even within this category, there are sub-kinds with unique traits:

A. Strict Genuine Customers

These customers are meticulous and firm in their expectations. They demand perfection and do not tolerate deviations from their standards. While they may make life challenging due to their high expectations, they remain genuine and committed to their values. They refuse bribery and expect the same level of integrity from others. Dealing with them pushes us to improve and adhere to a high standard of work. Despite their strict nature, their fairness and honesty make them reliable partners.

B. Lenient Genuine Customers

Lenient genuine customers share similarities with their strict counterparts in that they are systematic and committed to their values. However, they offer a level of flexibility when approached respectfully and with valid reasons. They are calm, composed, and more willing to listen, making them easier to engage with. They are patient and guide others to meet their expectations, fostering an environment of mutual growth and understanding.

C. Pretenders - Like Genuine Customers

This sub-type appears to be genuine on the surface but hides ulterior motives. They project an image of honesty and commitment but will only remain loyal as long as their needs are being met. Once a better opportunity arises, they will abandon previous commitments. These individuals can be particularly dangerous as they initially inspire trust but eventually prove to be toxic. Identifying and managing relationships with such individuals requires vigilance and strategic thinking to avoid potential harm.

2. Toxic Customers

Toxic customers pose significant challenges due to their self-serving and often destructive nature. While genuine customers contribute positively to relationships, toxic customers can erode trust and stability. The sub-kinds within this category include:

A. Direct Toxic Customers

These individuals display their negative traits openly and without shame. They are demanding and difficult to engage with as they prioritize their needs above all else. Direct toxic customers show little to no consideration for others' opinions and can be relentless in pursuing their goals. Handling such customers requires clear boundaries and firm management to avoid potential damage.

B. Indirect Toxic Customers

These individuals are more subtle in their approach but equally harmful. They often appear caring and supportive but are highly self-centred and manipulative. They gather information under the guise of concern, only to use it for personal gain. While they may not make direct demands, they expect to be accommodated, and failing to meet their unspoken expectations can lead to significant challenges. Managing interactions with indirect toxic customers requires careful observation and assertive communication.

C. Pretenders - Like Toxic Customers

Interestingly, this sub-type pretends to be toxic but ultimately has positive intentions. They may come across as harsh or demanding, but their actions are aimed at helping others grow. These individuals use tough love as a strategy to challenge and strengthen those around them. Although their approach can be perceived as rude or harsh, understanding their true intentions reveals their supportive nature. They do not seek personal gain but rather the improvement and success of those they care about.

Navigating Customer Relationships

Recognizing the type of customer we are dealing with—whether genuine or toxic—enables us to approach relationships with the appropriate strategies. Genuine customers can be trusted and foster growth, but even among them, vigilance is needed to identify pretenders. Toxic customers, on the other hand, require clear boundaries and thoughtful management to minimize potential harm.

In personal life, understanding these customer types helps us build healthier and more supportive connections, ensuring that we maintain our peace of mind and mutual respect. In professional life, effectively managing customer relationships is essential for maintaining a positive and productive work environment. The ability to identify, adapt, and respond to different customer types can lead to more successful and fulfilling interactions.

Descriptions and Examples for Each Customer Type

Genuine Customers:

Strict Genuine Customers: Consider an example of a project manager who consistently adheres to timelines, quality standards, and procedural requirements. If there's even a small deviation from the agreed plan, they are quick to point it out and demand corrections. While this can create stress, the benefit of working with them is that they drive excellence and foster a disciplined work culture. For instance, a supplier working for such a client might learn to improve quality checks, reducing future errors and boosting their reputation.

Lenient Genuine Customers: Picture a loyal client who appreciates the relationship and understands the complexities of a project. They set high expectations but are more willing to accommodate minor adjustments when informed in advance. An IT consultant working with such a customer may find that clear communication earns trust and builds a strong partnership over time.

Pretenders Who Seem Genuine: Imagine a colleague who always appears enthusiastic and supportive, participating in meetings with a positive attitude and seemingly upholding company values. However, as soon as an opportunity arises that benefits them personally, they pivot, prioritizing their gain over the team's needs. Identifying such behaviours requires keen observation and careful analysis of actions over time.

Toxic Customers:

Direct Toxic Customers: A CEO who disregards respectful communication and makes unreasonable demands is an example. They may send aggressive emails or voice complaints loudly during meetings, regardless of the quality of service provided. Handling these customers requires a resilient mindset and clear boundary-setting techniques.

Indirect Toxic Customers: Think of a department head who, on the surface, expresses concern for the team's welfare but subtly manipulates situations to their benefit. They might take credit for a subordinate's successful project while presenting it as teamwork. These customers can erode trust and morale if their tactics go unnoticed.

Pretenders Who Seem Toxic: Picture a strict mentor whose initial approach feels harsh and overly critical. They seem challenging to work with, but as time passes, it becomes evident that their feedback and stringent measures aim to push others to their potential. Understanding the intent behind their actions can shift the perception of these "toxic" individuals.

2. Strategies for Managing Each Customer Type

Approach for Strict Genuine Customers:

Be Meticulous: Always deliver precise, quality work. Ensure all promises are kept and backed up with proof, such as project documentation and quality checks.

Stay Proactive: Communicate potential issues ahead of time, allowing for problem-solving discussions before they escalate.

Approach for Lenient Genuine Customers:

Maintain Open Communication: Regularly update them on progress. They value transparency and will appreciate knowing where things stand.

Ask for Feedback: Since they are approachable, involve them in discussions to ensure alignment with their vision.

Approach for Pretenders Who Seem Genuine:

Observe Carefully: Look beyond words. Do they follow through on promises, or do they only appear committed when convenient?

Set Boundaries: Maintain a professional distance until their true intentions are clear.

Approach for Direct Toxic Customers:

Assertiveness is Key: Set clear boundaries without matching their confrontational energy. Use phrases like, "I understand your concern, and here's how we can address it."

Document Everything: Maintain records of interactions and agreements to protect against sudden shifts or accusations.

Approach for Indirect Toxic Customers:

Protect Your Ideas: Share information selectively and ensure credit is attributed properly.

Stay Neutral: Avoid being influenced by their charm or seemingly supportive attitude. Base interactions on facts and accountability.

Approach for Pretenders Who Seem Toxic:

Listen and Learn: Even if their approach seems rough, pay attention to the wisdom behind their critique.

Clarify Intentions: Engage them in conversations to understand their motivations, which can reveal their genuine concern for improvement.

3. Psychological Insights and Motivation

Understanding Genuine Customers:

Psychological Traits: Genuine customers value integrity and loyalty. They have strong ethical compasses, and their commitment is usually unwavering.

Motivation: Their primary motivation is reliability and achieving mutual success. They derive satisfaction from being part of trustworthy, productive relationships.

Understanding Toxic Customers:

Psychological Traits: Toxic customers often operate from a place of insecurity, self-interest, or a need for control. Their behaviour may stem from past experiences that taught them to prioritize self-preservation.

Motivation: They are driven by personal gain, power, or recognition. Understanding these motives can help tailor communication and strategies for smoother interactions.

4. Impact on Personal and Professional Life

Positive Impact of Genuine Customers: They contribute to a productive environment and teach valuable lessons in discipline, honesty, and accountability. Working with them helps develop resilience and adaptability.

Negative Impact of Toxic Customers: These relationships can lead to stress, burnout, and reduced morale. Personal and professional growth can stagnate if toxic behaviours dominate the work environment.

Mitigating Negative Impacts: Building emotional intelligence and resilience can buffer against the effects of toxic interactions. Engaging in regular self-reflection and mindfulness can also foster a more balanced approach.

5. Red Flags and Warning Signs

Identifying Toxic Pretenders:

Look for discrepancies between their words and actions.

Watch for inconsistent behaviour—being supportive when it benefits them but critical or disengaged otherwise.

Spotting Genuine Pretenders:

These individuals often have moments of genuine care that break through their harsh exterior. Pay attention to their actions during times of crisis or high pressure.

6. Tools for Self-Reflection and Boundary-Setting

Journaling: Reflect daily or weekly on customer interactions to identify patterns and adapt strategies accordingly.

Role-Playing: Practice conversations with a colleague or mentor to build confidence in setting boundaries and responding to toxic behaviours.

7. Identifying and Approaching Genuine and Toxic Customers

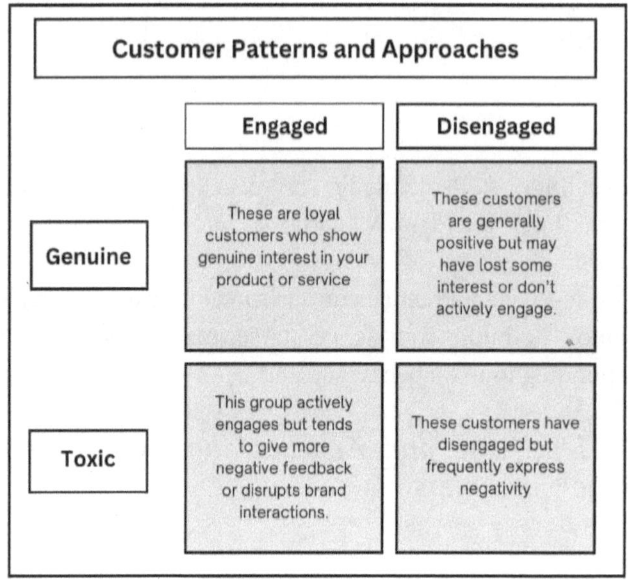

8. Customer Patterns and Approaches

Genuine, Engaged

Description: These customers are loyal and deeply interested in your product or service. They often provide constructive feedback, share their enthusiasm, and enhance the brand's image by positively contributing to its community.

Approach: Engage with these customers meaningfully. Encourage their feedback, reward their loyalty with exclusive insights or perks, and recognize their support publicly when possible. Building relationships with these customers strengthens brand loyalty and creates brand ambassadors who will naturally advocate for your business.

Handling Genuine, Engaged Customers: These customers are invaluable assets to any business, not only because they are loyal but also because they often serve as brand advocates, spreading positive word-of-mouth that attracts new customers. One of the biggest pitfalls, however, is assuming that these customers will remain loyal indefinitely simply because they're satisfied now.

Every interaction with a genuine, engaged customer should feel personalized and special, reinforcing their importance to your products, services, and overall approach. Acknowledging their past feedback, addressing them by name, and remembering their preferences demonstrate the level of care that makes them feel seen and valued. Offering exclusive benefits—such as early access to new products, invite-only events, or special discounts—further deepens their loyalty, making them feel like VIPs and keeping their experience with the brand fresh and exciting.

Regular communication is also essential, but it needs to be meaningful. Reaching out during quiet periods to thank them or check in without a sales agenda shows genuine interest, while responsiveness to their feedback reassures them that their voice is both heard and respected.

Genuine, engaged customers provide valuable insights for improving products and services, and by implementing their feedback, you can strengthen their connection to your brand even further. It's also crucial to address mistakes proactively—however small they may seem—since such customers have a vested interest in the brand's success. A quick, sincere apology and an offer to make things right can actually reinforce their loyalty, showing that the brand takes accountability seriously. Because engaged customers are often motivated by an emotional connection with the brand, it's important to cultivate this bond continuously. Small gestures, such as celebrating their milestones or sending thank-you notes, demonstrate that they're genuinely valued members of the brand community, not just customers. By approaching them with this consistent attention and appreciation, the risk of them feeling neglected or taking their loyalty for granted is minimized, reducing the chance that they might disengage over time.

One of the most common yet subtle mistakes in managing relationships with genuine, engaged customers is allowing the connection to become overly personal or too intimate. While building rapport and fostering closeness are key to strengthening loyalty, crossing certain boundaries can risk cultivating an unprofessional familiarity that may ultimately backfire. When the lines between a professional and a personal relationship blur, it can inadvertently create expectations and emotional entanglements that may lead to misunderstandings. These customers may begin to feel entitled to preferential treatment or may become disappointed over minor issues, as the closeness can amplify any perceived slights. This is where ego often comes into play: too much familiarity may lead the customer to expect special handling, which can cause strain if their expectations aren't met or if a boundary is enforced.

Genuine, Disengaged

Description: Generally supportive, these customers may have disengaged over time due to changing needs or shifting priorities. They're often receptive to re-engagement if prompted but may require a compelling reason to re-establish connection.

Approach: Re-engage these customers through personalized marketing efforts, check-ins, and reminders.

Consider incentives like special offers, new product releases, or a loyalty program to renew their interest. Showing genuine interest in their needs and addressing any potential dissatisfaction can rekindle their engagement.

Handling Genuine, Disengaged Customers: Genuine disengaged customers are a crucial segment that deserves focused attention, as re-engaging them can be instrumental to strengthening the customer base and driving growth. These customers may have once been enthusiastic and committed to the brand but, for various reasons, have drifted away from active engagement. The first step to winning back these customers lies in a deep understanding of their unique needs and expectations. This requires an active effort to listen, observe, and empathize with their potential concerns, motivations, and reasons for disengagement.

It's essential to carefully analyse if any aspect of the product, service, or communication has fallen short or caused frustration. There may be subtle factors, such as unaddressed concerns, overlooked feedback, or even minor service lapses, which these customers may have found disappointing but haven't openly communicated. By identifying these underlying issues, we can address potential pain points and make improvements to create a more fulfilling experience. Regular feedback collection, personalized outreach, and showing genuine interest in understanding their preferences can all signal to them that their satisfaction is highly valued.

Converting disengaged customers back into engaged advocates is not only valuable for retaining their loyalty but also for strengthening the brand's reputation and credibility. Every re-engaged customer serves as a testament to the business's commitment to continuous improvement and customer-centricity. By refining products, services, or approaches based on this feedback, businesses become more adaptable, responsive, and aligned with customer needs. This process ultimately makes the brand more resilient and fosters an environment where growth becomes not only achievable but also sustainable in the long term.

Toxic, Engaged

Description: These customers are highly engaged but often critical, voicing frequent complaints or negative opinions. They can affect other customers' experiences by creating tension or dampening positivity within community spaces.
Approach: Acknowledge their feedback professionally and address any valid concerns. Set boundaries to prevent negativity from overtaking interactions with other customers. By addressing genuine concerns without overly indulging in unconstructive complaints, you can maintain a positive environment while offering respectful responses.

Handling Toxic, Engaged Customers: These customers are a challenging yet potentially transformative segment. While these customers may consistently interact with the brand, their engagement often comes with negative feedback, disruptive comments, or a general tendency to voice dissatisfaction. Despite this, their continuous engagement indicates a level of investment in the product or service, suggesting that, with careful handling, there may be opportunities to shift their relationship from contentious to constructive. The first step in addressing this group is to conduct a detailed analysis of why their engagement tends toward toxicity. It's critical to understand whether their negativity stems from personal preferences, unmet expectations, or perhaps previous experiences that haven't been fully addressed.

Engaging an external consultant or team with expertise in customer behaviour analysis can provide an unbiased, objective assessment of these customers. Specialists can help distinguish between customers who may naturally lean toward critical or difficult interactions and those whose grievances may stem from valid, resolvable issues. This outside perspective can also offer insights into patterns of behaviour, identifying if their concerns reflect broader areas of improvement within the product, service, or communication strategies. For instance, external consultants may pinpoint recurring themes in feedback, helping the brand prioritize improvements that could appease not only the toxic customers but also positively impact the wider customer base. This feedback loop allows for meaningful adjustments that elevate overall customer satisfaction and experience.

If feasible, the ultimate goal would be to transform these toxic but engaged customers into genuinely satisfied advocates. Converting someone from critical to loyal can be immensely rewarding and can generate positive word-of-mouth for the brand, as their journey toward satisfaction demonstrates the business's commitment to growth and customer care. Through constructive engagement, responsive communication, and a willingness to address genuine concerns, these customers might recognize the brand's dedication to improvement. Success in this conversion not only bolsters brand reputation but also showcases adaptability and resilience, reinforcing the value of customer-focused growth.

Toxic, Disengaged

Description: These customers have mostly disengaged from your brand, occasionally voicing negativity but showing little interest in any meaningful engagement. Their loyalty is low, and they are unlikely to convert back to active customers.

Approach: Limit engagement with these customers to essential interactions only, focusing your energy on constructive customer relationships. If valid feedback emerges, take it into account, but avoid expending resources on prolonged follow-ups. This allows you to focus efforts on customers who contribute positively to the brand.

Handling Toxic, Disengaged Customers: These customers represent a segment that, while distant, carries the potential for significant disruption if actively re-engaged. These customers often have minimal investment in the brand or product, yet they may occasionally voice negativity or criticism. Unlike actively engaged toxic customers, they are typically unresponsive and show no commitment to any improvement or resolution. Attempting to retain or reconnect with them can often lead to unnecessary complications, diverting valuable time and resources away from more productive relationships.

The best approach with toxic disengaged customers is often to maintain a respectful distance. Investing effort in customers who are fundamentally unaligned with the brand can lead to a cycle of unproductive interactions, with feedback that is rarely constructive or actionable. In some cases, efforts to re-engage them may even fuel further negativity, creating a sense of frustration for the customer and the team. By focusing on nurturing genuinely engaged and constructive customers, the business can maintain a more positive and encouraging environment for both staff and clients.

This doesn't mean ignoring all feedback from disengaged customers entirely, but it is essential to recognize when their impact on the company culture, staff morale, and day-to-day operations outweighs any potential benefits. Instead, prioritizing efforts toward more responsive and loyal customers allows the business to flourish in a balanced, growth-oriented way. Letting go of relationships that add strain or complication not only preserves resources but helps cultivate a community of engaged, satisfied customers who align with the business's values and vision.

CHAPTER THIRTEEN

Handling Customers

The notion that "customers are always correct" may sound appealing and promote customer satisfaction, but it introduces a form of partiality. In reality, customers can make mistakes. Genuine customers are those who recognize and admit their mistakes, working collaboratively toward a solution. Toxic customers, on the other hand, often acknowledge their errors internally but refuse to admit them, choosing instead to project blame elsewhere.

Understanding Customer Dynamics

In daily interactions, we will encounter both genuine and toxic customers. The key to managing these relationships lies in our preparedness to handle any challenges with positivity and resilience. Ensuring that mistakes are identified, addressed, and corrected is not just about resolving present issues; it is a foundational step in preventing future conflicts. This responsibility extends beyond individual actions and should be passed down to successors and team members.

In professional settings, genuine customers take accountability for their missteps and collaborate on solutions. Conversely, toxic customers conceal their errors and deflect blame. Establishing clear processes and approaches can minimize confusion and create a transparent environment.

1. Communication

Timely and effective communication is essential. When problems arise, immediate attention is required. Delaying communication sends a message of negligence and weakness, which can damage credibility. Leaders, in both personal and professional spheres, must address issues as soon as they occur.

Communication must be approached with a positive, ethical, and principled mindset. Even in difficult situations, this standard should not waver. By maintaining integrity in communication, long-term, sustainable solutions can be achieved. Approaches rooted in partiality or superficial fixes only serve to delay consequences that can later become destructive, undermining everything built over time.

The Johari Window Model

Integrating the Johari Window communication model into our practices provides significant insight. This model, which includes four quadrants, can help identify known and unknown aspects between ourselves and our customers:

1. Open Area: What both we and our customers know.

2. Hidden Area: Information we know but our customers do not.

3. Blind Area: What our customers know that we do not.

4. Unknown Area: What neither party knows.

Expanding our "Open Area" builds trust and transparency, fostering better communication. This transparency is invaluable in recognizing and resolving problems.

Focusing on the Person

When dealing with customer issues, our initial focus should be on the individual communicating the problem, not just the problem itself. Addressing the person first builds trust and creates an environment where solutions can be effectively discussed. Many times, organizations focus solely on problem resolution without understanding the emotional and psychological needs of the customer, which can lead to dissatisfaction even if the issue is technically resolved.

The Importance of Listening

Listening is a critical component of handling any customer interaction. We must allow the individual to express themselves fully, including any anger, frustration, or concerns. This uninterrupted space not only validates their feelings but also provides insight into the problem's root causes. Listening without interjecting or defending oneself requires patience and humility, traits that are indispensable in both personal and professional life.

Sincere Apologies

Apologies should be heartfelt and genuine. A superficial apology will only exacerbate the problem, making the individual feel misunderstood or undervalued. Saying "I am sorry" should not be a mere formality but a reflection of genuine empathy and a willingness to take responsibility. The customer must feel that their pain or inconvenience has been acknowledged. This approach fosters goodwill and demonstrates that we prioritize relationships over mere transactions.

Communication with Manners and Integrity

Every interaction, regardless of the pressure or stakes involved, must be conducted with manners and integrity. Maintaining respect and ethical conduct during conversations sets a standard of excellence and fairness. When customers see that we are committed to solving their issues ethically, they are more likely to trust us and remain loyal.

Even when dealing with toxic customers, maintaining composure and adhering to ethical standards is crucial.

These customers may challenge our patience or push us to bend rules, but staying true to our principles will protect our reputation and peace of mind in the long term.

Transition from AI to AEI (Artificial and Emotional Intelligence)

As technology evolves, our interactions are enhanced by AI (Artificial Intelligence), which aids in solving technical issues and automating responses. However, when it comes to deeply human interactions, AEI (Artificial and Emotional Intelligence) is the next frontier. AEI would blend traditional AI capabilities with emotional understanding, offering insights into the emotional state of the customer and suggesting appropriate responses that resonate on a human level.

Imagine a system that not only recognizes customer frustration but also adapts the tone of its communication or suggests actions that convey empathy. While AI can provide quick solutions, AEI would ensure that these solutions are delivered with care, making the customer feel heard and valued.

Why Focus on the Person First?

Problems, no matter how severe, cannot think, feel, or empathize. They exist as static issues. It's the person facing the problem who brings emotion, context, and urgency to the situation. Addressing the individual's needs first humanizes the interaction. Showing empathy can de-escalate tension, creating a space where solutions can be more effectively communicated and implemented.

when we prioritize the person:

- We establish trust.
- We open the door for genuine dialogue.
- We create an environment where solutions can be received more openly.

Focusing on the Problem

Once the individual has been heard, and their concerns acknowledged, we can shift our focus to the actual problem. By separating the emotional aspect from the technical or procedural aspects of the issue, we can approach solutions more objectively.

Identifying the Causes and Reasons

Understanding the causes and reasons behind a problem is vital. Problems do not arise in a vacuum; they are often the result of multiple contributing factors. Identifying these factors helps us not only solve the current issue but also put preventive measures in place to avoid future occurrences.

1. Procedural Gaps: Sometimes, problems arise due to gaps in processes or systems. These gaps can lead to misunderstandings, errors, or inefficiencies. Regular process audits can help identify and close these gaps.

2. Human Error: Mistakes can occur at any level, from the customer to the service provider. Acknowledging human error and creating a culture where it can be admitted without fear of severe consequences encourages transparency and quicker resolutions.

3. Communication Breakdowns: Problems can often be traced back to unclear or incomplete communication. Ensuring that communication channels are clear, open, and accessible can prevent misunderstandings and facilitate better problem-solving.

4. Expectations vs. Reality: Customers may have expectations that differ from what can realistically be delivered. Understanding these discrepancies can help adjust processes or better set expectations in the future.

5. Technical Issues: At times, the problem is rooted in technical malfunctions or failures. Leveraging AI tools for troubleshooting and understanding these technical issues can expedite solutions, but AEI would enhance this by adapting responses to convey empathy alongside technical expertise.

Addressing the Problem Systematically

To ensure consistency and fairness when handling problems:

- Analyse Data: Use data from past interactions to understand patterns and identify common causes.
- Develop Solutions Collaboratively: Engage with both the team and the customer to come up with solutions that meet everyone's needs.

- Implement Preventative Measures: Once the issue is resolved, take steps to prevent recurrence. This may involve updating procedures, training staff, or upgrading technology.

The Role of Feedback and Audits

Feedback mechanisms are essential in refining how problems are approached and resolved. Periodic audits of problem-handling processes can reveal strengths and areas for improvement, ensuring that both genuine and toxic customers are managed effectively.

A Balanced Approach

Focusing on the person first and the problem second is the most effective way to ensure that customer interactions are not just transactional but relational. While advanced AI tools can aid in problem-solving, the future of handling complex interactions lies in adopting AEI, where emotional intelligence complements technical solutions.

2. Process & Systems

Handling customers effectively requires robust processes and systems in place. This ensures consistency and fairness, especially when differentiating between genuine and toxic customers. Process-driven approaches facilitate clear steps for addressing issues while maintaining customer trust.

Addressing the Problem

Before diving into problem-solving, it's essential to focus on the person, as mentioned earlier. Once the individual feels heard and respected, only then should we proceed to address the problem itself. An effective system incorporates:

- Documentation: Keeping a detailed record of interactions and outcomes to prevent future misunderstandings.
- Evaluation: Assessing how the problem was resolved and identifying areas for process improvement.
- Transparency: Sharing the steps taken and updates with the customer.

Toxic customers might exploit loopholes in the system or bypass processes to create confusion. Reinforcing procedures and ensuring all interactions are documented can safeguard against such issues.

3. Feedback Mechanisms

Feedback from customers, whether positive or negative, is an invaluable resource. It allows for continuous improvement and demonstrates a commitment to growth. For genuine customers, feedback may be willingly shared and used to strengthen the relationship. Toxic customers may be less forthcoming or manipulative with feedback, using it to exert control.

Listening Without Interrupting

When receiving feedback, practice active listening. Resist the urge to respond immediately. Allow customers to complete their thoughts, and then evaluate their points critically but constructively. This approach not only fosters goodwill but also helps identify actionable insights for improvement.

Feedback mechanisms should include:

• Surveys and Direct Feedback: Tools that gather customer insights regularly.

• Review Sessions: Meetings with team members to discuss and apply feedback.

• Action Plans: A strategy for implementing changes based on feedback, followed by communicating these changes to the customer.

4. Periodic Audits

Regularly auditing customer interactions, processes, and outcomes is essential for continuous improvement. These audits help identify gaps and ensure that both genuine and toxic customers are being managed effectively.

Benefits of Periodic Audits

• Consistency: Ensures all customers are treated fairly and in line with company values.

• Accountability: Holds teams responsible for their interactions and problem-solving approaches.

• Prevention: Helps spot recurring issues early and prevent them from escalating.

Audits should be transparent and shared with customers when appropriate. This reinforces trust and shows that feedback and interactions are taken seriously.

5. Upgradation as We Grow

Growth involves adapting and refining processes. As we evolve, so too should our approaches to handling customers. Upgrading systems, communication tools, and training ensures that we stay effective and efficient.

Implementing Change

Changes should be communicated transparently. Both genuine and toxic customers need to be aware of improvements that could affect them. For genuine customers, this might mean more streamlined services or better communication platforms. For toxic customers, it could signal that manipulative tactics will be less effective.

Upgrading approaches include:

• Training Programs: Continuous education for employees on how to manage different types of customers.

• Technology Integration: Using modern tools for better data collection and analysis.

• Customer Education: Informing customers about new features or practices that will benefit them.

Person First, Problem Second

In today's fast-paced business environment, the customer experience is paramount. To cultivate lasting relationships with customers, organizations must prioritize the individual behind the transaction, placing the person before the problem. This principle underscores the importance of empathy, effective communication, and integrity in fostering trust and loyalty. By embracing this mindset, businesses can navigate challenges more effectively and create a positive impact on their customers' lives.

Understanding the Importance of People-Centricity

At its core, the idea of placing the person first emphasizes recognizing that every customer is more than just a number or a complaint. They are individuals with unique experiences, emotions, and needs. When businesses acknowledge this, they can begin to tailor their interactions in ways that resonate deeply with their customers.

Empathy as a Foundation: Empathy is the ability to understand and share the feelings of another. In customer service, this means actively listening to customers and validating their emotions. When a customer expresses frustration or dissatisfaction, responding with empathy can diffuse tension and signal that their concerns are taken seriously. For instance, rather than merely addressing the technical aspects of a complaint, a representative might say, "I understand how frustrating this situation must be for you. Let's work together to find a solution." This approach acknowledges the customer's feelings and demonstrates that the business values them as individuals.

Genuine Communication: Effective communication goes beyond simply providing information. It involves engaging in a meaningful dialogue that fosters connection.

By employing active listening techniques and open-ended questions, businesses can better understand the customer's perspective and tailor their responses accordingly. For example, asking questions like, "Can you tell me more about your experience?" invites customers to share their stories, allowing representatives to address their needs more comprehensively.

Integrity in Actions: Integrity is crucial in building trust. Customers want to know that they can rely on a business to follow through on promises and commitments. When issues arise, it's essential for businesses to be transparent and honest about what went wrong and what steps will be taken to rectify the situation. Admitting mistakes and taking responsibility not only helps resolve issues but also reinforces the relationship with the customer.

Building Trust Through Person-Centric Interactions

Trust is the cornerstone of any successful relationship. By prioritizing the person over the problem, businesses can cultivate trust that leads to long-term loyalty. Here are some strategies to enhance trust-building efforts:

Personalized Experiences: Tailoring interactions to meet the specific needs and preferences of customers creates a sense of value and recognition. This can be achieved through customer relationship management (CRM) systems that track customer interactions, preferences, and feedback. For instance, a hotel that remembers a returning guest's preferences for room type or amenities demonstrates attentiveness and care, significantly enhancing the overall experience.

Empowerment and Agency: Allowing customers to have a say in how their issues are resolved empowers them and fosters a collaborative relationship. When customers feel involved in the decision-making process, they are more likely to feel satisfied with the outcome, even if the solution doesn't fully meet their expectations. For instance, providing options for resolution (e.g., a refund, replacement, or store credit) gives customers a sense of control and respect.

Proactive Outreach: Businesses should not wait for problems to arise before engaging with customers. Proactively reaching out to customers to solicit feedback or check in on their satisfaction can prevent issues from escalating and demonstrates a commitment to their well-being. This could take the form of follow-up calls, surveys, or personalized emails.

Handling Challenging Situations: Every business encounters challenging customers, but how these situations are handled can make a significant difference. By focusing on the person rather than the problem, representatives can de-escalate conflicts and turn negative experiences into opportunities for positive outcomes. For example, when dealing with an upset customer, acknowledging their feelings and offering sincere apologies can significantly change the course of the interaction, often leading to a more favourable resolution.

Transforming Challenges into Growth Opportunities

When businesses adopt a "Person First, Problem Second" approach, they not only address immediate issues but also lay the groundwork for future growth. By viewing challenges as learning opportunities, organizations can enhance their service delivery and foster resilience.

Reflective Practices: After resolving a customer issue, businesses can benefit from reflecting on the interaction. What worked well? What could have been handled differently? This introspection can inform future strategies and training programs, equipping teams to handle similar situations more effectively in the future.

Encouraging Customer Feedback: Inviting customers to provide feedback on their experiences allows businesses to identify trends and areas for improvement. Feedback is a valuable tool that can inform product development, service enhancements, and overall business strategy. Moreover, it shows customers that their opinions matter and that the business is committed to continuous improvement.

Training and Development: Investing in employee training that emphasizes empathy, communication skills, and problem-solving fosters a culture that prioritizes the customer. When employees are equipped with the tools to engage meaningfully with customers, they are more likely to create positive experiences that build long-term loyalty.

A Vital Approach to Enhancing Relationships and Fostering Loyalty

Placing the person before the problem is not merely a customer service philosophy; it is a vital approach that enhances relationships and fosters loyalty. By prioritizing empathy, genuine communication, and integrity, businesses can transform challenging interactions into opportunities for growth and trust-building. Ultimately, this person-centric mindset enriches both personal and professional experiences, paving the way for lasting success in a competitive marketplace.

At The End: Embracing Respect, Empathy, And Growth

As we conclude Balancing Customer Expectations – The Truth Unveiled, it's vital to reflect on the transformative power of treating everyone we encounter with the dignity and attention they deserve. This mindset, which extends beyond the confines of customer service, is a guiding principle for living a fulfilling and harmonious life. The idea that everyone is, in essence, a 'customer' reminds us to approach interactions with patience, kindness, and an open heart—qualities that transcend professional gain and enrich our personal experiences.

Throughout this book, we explored how respectful communication, emotional resilience, and empathy can help us navigate challenges with grace. Adopting these practices encourages a shift in perspective, allowing us to see obstacles as opportunities for connection and growth. This journey is not without its trials, as it demands consistent effort and introspection, but the outcome is worth it: a life built on meaningful relationships and a legacy of positive influence.

By incorporating these insights into our daily lives, we contribute to an environment where understanding and mutual respect are paramount. Let us commit to these values, ensuring our actions reflect the best of who we are and inspire those around us. As we move forward, may we continue to grow, led by example, and be remembered not just for our successes, but for how we made others feel—valued, heard, and respected.

Exploring The Core Of The Book

The notion that "customers are always correct" may sound appealing and promote customer satisfaction, but it introduces a form of partiality. In reality, customers can make mistakes. Genuine customers are those who recognize and admit their mistakes, working collaboratively toward a solution. Toxic customers, on the other hand, often acknowledge their errors internally but refuse to admit them, choosing instead to project blame elsewhere.

Understanding Customer Dynamics

In daily interactions, we will encounter both genuine and toxic customers. The key to managing these relationships lies in our preparedness to handle any challenges with positivity and resilience. Ensuring that mistakes are identified, addressed, and corrected is not just about resolving present issues; it is a foundational step in preventing future conflicts. This responsibility extends beyond individual actions and should be passed down to successors and team members.

In professional settings, genuine customers take accountability for their missteps and collaborate on solutions. Conversely, toxic customers conceal their errors and deflect blame. Establishing clear processes and approaches can minimize confusion and create a transparent environment.

1. Communication

Timely and effective communication is essential. When problems arise, immediate attention is required. Delaying communication sends a message of negligence and weakness, which can damage credibility. Leaders, in both personal and professional spheres, must address issues as soon as they occur.

Communication must be approached with a positive, ethical, and principled mindset. Even in difficult situations, this standard should not waver. By maintaining integrity in communication, long-term, sustainable solutions can be achieved. Approaches rooted in partiality or superficial fixes only serve to delay consequences that can later become destructive, undermining everything built over time.

The Johari Window Model

Integrating the Johari Window communication model into our practices provides significant insight. This model, which includes four quadrants, can help identify known and unknown aspects between ourselves and our customers:

1. Open Area: What both we and our customers know.
2. Hidden Area: Information we know but our customers do not.
3. Blind Area: What our customers know that we do not.
4. Unknown Area: What neither party knows.

Expanding our "Open Area" builds trust and transparency, fostering better communication. This transparency is invaluable in recognizing and resolving problems.

Focusing on the Person

When dealing with customer issues, our initial focus should be on the individual communicating the problem, not just the problem itself. Addressing the person first builds trust and creates an environment where solutions can be effectively discussed. Many times, organizations focus solely on problem resolution without understanding the emotional and psychological needs of the customer, which can lead to dissatisfaction even if the issue is technically resolved.

The Importance of Listening

Listening is a critical component of handling any customer interaction. We must allow the individual to express themselves fully, including any anger, frustration, or concerns. This uninterrupted space not only validates their feelings but also provides insight into the problem's root causes. Listening without interjecting or defending oneself requires patience and humility, traits that are indispensable in both personal and professional life.

Sincere Apologies

Apologies should be heartfelt and genuine. A superficial apology will only exacerbate the problem, making the individual feel misunderstood or undervalued. Saying "I am sorry" should not be a mere formality but a reflection of genuine empathy and a willingness to take responsibility. The customer must feel that their pain or inconvenience has been acknowledged. This approach fosters goodwill and demonstrates that we prioritize relationships over mere transactions.

Communication with Manners and Integrity

Every interaction, regardless of the pressure or stakes involved, must be conducted with manners and integrity.

Maintaining respect and ethical conduct during conversations sets a standard of excellence and fairness. When customers see that we are committed to solving their issues ethically, they are more likely to trust us and remain loyal.

Even when dealing with toxic customers, maintaining composure and adhering to ethical standards is crucial. These customers may challenge our patience or push us to bend rules, but staying true to our principles will protect our reputation and peace of mind in the long term.

Transition from AI to AEI (Artificial and Emotional Intelligence)

As technology evolves, our interactions are enhanced by AI (Artificial Intelligence), which aids in solving technical issues and automating responses. However, when it comes to deeply human interactions, AEI (Artificial and Emotional Intelligence) is the next frontier. AEI would blend traditional AI capabilities with emotional understanding, offering insights into the emotional state of the customer and suggesting appropriate responses that resonate on a human level.

Imagine a system that not only recognizes customer frustration but also adapts the tone of its communication or suggests actions that convey empathy. While AI can provide quick solutions, AEI would ensure that these solutions are delivered with care, making the customer feel heard and valued.

Why Focus on the Person First?

Problems, no matter how severe, cannot think, feel, or empathize. They exist as static issues. It's the person facing the problem who brings emotion, context, and urgency to the situation. Addressing the individual's needs first humanizes the interaction. Showing empathy can de-escalate tension, creating a space where solutions can be more effectively communicated and implemented.

when we prioritize the person:

• We establish trust.

• We open the door for genuine dialogue.

• We create an environment where solutions can be received more openly.

Focusing on the Problem

Once the individual has been heard, and their concerns acknowledged, we can shift our focus to the actual problem. By separating the emotional aspect from the technical or procedural aspects of the issue, we can approach solutions more objectively.

Identifying the Causes and Reasons

Understanding the causes and reasons behind a problem is vital. Problems do not arise in a vacuum; they are often the result of multiple contributing factors. Identifying these factors helps us not only solve the current issue but also put preventive measures in place to avoid future occurrences.

1. Procedural Gaps: Sometimes, problems arise due to gaps in processes or systems. These gaps can lead to misunderstandings, errors, or inefficiencies. Regular process audits can help identify and close these gaps.

2. Human Error: Mistakes can occur at any level, from the customer to the service provider. Acknowledging human error and creating a culture where it can be admitted without fear of severe consequences encourages transparency and quicker resolutions.

3. Communication Breakdowns: Problems can often be traced back to unclear or incomplete communication. Ensuring that communication channels are clear, open, and accessible can prevent misunderstandings and facilitate

better problem-solving.

4. Expectations vs. Reality: Customers may have expectations that differ from what can realistically be delivered. Understanding these discrepancies can help adjust processes or better set expectations in the future.

5. Technical Issues: At times, the problem is rooted in technical malfunctions or failures. Leveraging AI tools for troubleshooting and understanding these technical issues can expedite solutions, but AEI would enhance this by adapting responses to convey empathy alongside technical expertise.

Addressing the Problem Systematically

To ensure consistency and fairness when handling problems:

- Analyse Data: Use data from past interactions to understand patterns and identify common causes.
- Develop Solutions Collaboratively: Engage with both the team and the customer to come up with solutions that meet everyone's needs.
- Implement Preventative Measures: Once the issue is resolved, take steps to prevent recurrence. This may involve updating procedures, training staff, or upgrading technology.

The Role of Feedback and Audits

Feedback mechanisms are essential in refining how problems are approached and resolved. Periodic audits of problem-handling processes can reveal strengths and areas for improvement, ensuring that both genuine and toxic customers are managed effectively.

A Balanced Approach

Focusing on the person first and the problem second is the most effective way to ensure that customer interactions are not just transactional but relational. While advanced

AI tools can aid in problem-solving, the future of handling complex interactions lies in adopting AEI, where emotional intelligence complements technical solutions.

2. Process & Systems

Handling customers effectively requires robust processes and systems in place. This ensures consistency and fairness, especially when differentiating between genuine and toxic customers. Process-driven approaches facilitate clear steps for addressing issues while maintaining customer trust.

Addressing the Problem

Before diving into problem-solving, it's essential to focus on the person, as mentioned earlier. Once the individual feels heard and respected, only then should we proceed to address the problem itself. An effective system incorporates:

- Documentation: Keeping a detailed record of interactions and outcomes to prevent future misunderstandings.
- Evaluation: Assessing how the problem was resolved and identifying areas for process improvement.
- Transparency: Sharing the steps taken and updates with the customer.

Toxic customers might exploit loopholes in the system or bypass processes to create confusion. Reinforcing procedures and ensuring all interactions are documented can safeguard against such issues.

3. Feedback Mechanisms

Feedback from customers, whether positive or negative, is an invaluable resource. It allows for continuous improvement and demonstrates a commitment to growth. For genuine customers, feedback may be willingly shared and used to strengthen the relationship. Toxic customers may be less forthcoming or manipulative with feedback, using it to exert control.

Listening Without Interrupting

When receiving feedback, practice active listening. Resist the urge to respond immediately. Allow customers to complete their thoughts, and then evaluate their points critically but constructively. This approach not only fosters goodwill but also helps identify actionable insights for improvement.

Feedback mechanisms should include:

- Surveys and Direct Feedback: Tools that gather customer insights regularly.
- Review Sessions: Meetings with team members to discuss and apply feedback.
- Action Plans: A strategy for implementing changes based on feedback, followed by communicating these changes to the customer.

4. Periodic Audits

Regularly auditing customer interactions, processes, and outcomes is essential for continuous improvement. These audits help identify gaps and ensure that both genuine and toxic customers are being managed effectively.

Benefits of Periodic Audits

• Consistency: Ensures all customers are treated fairly and in line with company values.

• Accountability: Holds teams responsible for their interactions and problem-solving approaches.

• Prevention: Helps spot recurring issues early and prevent them from escalating.

Audits should be transparent and shared with customers when appropriate. This reinforces trust and shows that feedback and interactions are taken seriously.

5. Upgradation as We Grow

Growth involves adapting and refining processes. As we evolve, so too should our approaches to handling customers. Upgrading systems, communication tools, and training ensures that we stay effective and efficient.

Implementing Change

Changes should be communicated transparently. Both genuine and toxic customers need to be aware of improvements that could affect them. For genuine customers, this might mean more streamlined services or better communication platforms. For toxic customers, it could signal that manipulative tactics will be less effective.

Upgrading approaches include:

• Training Programs: Continuous education for employees on how to manage different types of customers.

• Technology Integration: Using modern tools for better data collection and analysis.

• Customer Education: Informing customers about new features or practices that will benefit them.

Person First, Problem Second

To maintain a successful, long-term relationship with customers, it is essential to address the person before the problem. Empathy, genuine communication, and integrity are critical. By focusing on the person involved and treating each interaction as an opportunity to build trust, we pave the way for stronger relationships—even with the most challenging customers.

www.ingramcontent.com/pod-product-compliance
Lightning Source LLC
La Vergne TN
LVHW041105150826
845673LV00007B/1936

* 9 7 9 8 8 9 6 1 0 4 3 8 4 *